The M̲... of A̲...

Ann Walker

C000150532

www.capallbann.co.uk

The Mystic Life of Animals

©1998 Ann Walker

ISBN 186163 0166

First printed 1998
Reprinted 2003

ALL RIGHTS RESERVED

No part of this publication may be reproduced, stored in a retrieval system or transmitted in any form or by any means, electronic, mechanical, photocopying, scanning, recording or otherwise without the prior written permission of the author and the publisher.

Cover design by Paul Mason

Published by:

Capall Bann Publishing
Auton Farm
Milverton
Somerset
TA4 1NE

Dedication

For St. Francis - A saint for the 21st. century

Also by the author, published by Capall Bann:

Living Tarot
Your Talking Pet
Cats' Company
Intuitive Journey

Contents

St Francis

Great men care for little things;
Only the small dare not.
St. Francis loved each bird that sings,
And knew each special plot
Where tiny flowers their faces turned
To Brother Sun and Sister Rain.
No living thing was ever spurned,
He lived for love and not for gain.

Birds and Beasts as well as Man
Were loved and nurtured, taught
And preached to, for in God's plan
We're one complete and Holy Thought.
And when at death his soul left Earth
His friends, the larks, on myriad wings,
Saluted him who knew the worth
Of many splendoured little things.

Ann Walker

Chapter One

Them & Us - or Are We All One?

Communication is the golden key that unlocks the door to understanding. Man has channelled almost all forms of communication into some form or other of speech. We have developed this to the detriment of our other senses, our other forms of communication. Even writing after all is just another form of speech, the use of words.

We have such sophisticated forms of communication involving speech, the telephone, radio, television. It is possible now for almost anyone, almost anywhere, to speak to another person even if they are on the other side of the world. Because we have this technical ability we are apt to think that the animals, who do not possess this know-how, have little or no means of communication. How wrong we are in that assumption.

Because animals are not, as we like to say, cerebral creatures like us most of their communication is on what could be termed a solar plexus level. This means they are concerned with emotions, feelings, events and happenings in the here and now.

Animals communicate very clearly the basic emotions, fear, anger, love etc, not only to one another but to us – if we are receptive enough to receive them. They are receiving these messages from us all the time.

Unfortunately we tend to view communication with the animal world in forms of radio in which we are the transmitters and the animal is the receiver. Communication to be successful has to be a two-way thing, we have to learn to receive as well as transmit. This so often means just being, listening, watching and learning. If we take any form of successful (in our eyes) communication between man and animal, the rider and his horse, the shepherd and his dog for instance, it is the animal who has received and learned the words, the signals etc, that the man has chosen to transmit.

A lifetime of living with and loving animals has brought me to the conclusion that a great deal of animal communication is what I would call direct 'mind to mind' communication. Explained in simple terms, animals 'see' something with their mind's eye as a clear picture, rather like a colour slide projected on a screen. This somehow is projected, just like the colour slide, into another mind and so the message is delivered.

This is not, of course, the only way animals communicate one with another and with us. They use their voices – many animals have quite a wide range of vocal sounds, and they use body language a great deal; particularly ear and tail movements. They also seem to communicate by some form of close nose-to-nose breathing. Many animals will, as we say, 'sniff noses' and in the sniffing apparently communicate some message.

Barbara Woodhouse, well-known not only as a dog-trainer but for her ability to train horses, relates in one of her books how she learned the secret of breathing up a horse's nostrils to tame it from an Indian horse-trainer while living in South America.

But back to our direct mind-to-mind communication. My belief in this form of communication stems from personal experience. I have from time to time received messages from animals this way. They have always been totally unexpected, but extremely clear. The first time I can ever remember this happening it probably saved me from serious injury or worse.

I was in my mid-teens at the time and at a small country horse show in England with my pony. I had left her hitched to the fence pulling hay from her net and had gone to watch the Open Jumping competition which was taking place in the ring. The ground was soft and wet after recent rain and the large bay horse just doing his round slipped on take-off, blundered through one of the jumps, falling on one knee and unseating his rider.

Frightened by the bits of jump rolling around his feet and the over-enthusiastic stewards who ran forward to catch him, arms akimbo, he galloped for the exit. Here more arm-waving men barred his way. Now thoroughly alarmed he galloped round the ring looking for another way out.

The crowd were two or three deep all round the ropes, except where I was standing. Although I had people close each side of me there was no-one directly behind me. I saw him galloping straight towards me; for some reason I couldn't move (I was literally, as I have often read of other people being, 'rooted to the spot!'). Then for a split second his face was directly in front of me, his eyes it seemed were looking into mine and quite clearly in my mind I had a picture of myself ducking and the horse going over me. Without hesitation, I ducked, felt the wind as the big horse, hoofs neatly tucked up, went over, then the soft thud as he landed on the turf just behind me.

My father, who saw the whole incident, rushed up full of congratulations for my 'presence of mind'. "Whatever made you duck - if you'd moved he would have landed on you" he exclaimed. No wonder he was surprised, I was myself, I had never been renowned for keeping cool, calm and collected in emergencies. All I could do was reply "I don't know - I just knew he was going to jump" I felt that to add, "he told me so", would have been stretching the credulity of my father, great animal lover though he was, too much.

Since then I have experienced this direct mind-to-mind communication many times with different animals, but never with such a dramatic message as this. In fact they have always been very ordinary communications and have come when least expected. I must emphasise here that this type of communication with an animal is totally different from the day to day understanding by observing the look in the animal's eye, the sounds it makes, it's attitude and actions and thus knowing what it is feeling. This mind-to-mind business is instantaneous and very definite. More often than not it happens with animals with which one has a very close affinity. A good example of this was Debbie.

Debbie was one of my donkeys, and to me a very special one. As a tiny foal, only a couple of weeks old she was struck down with a mystery sickness. There were no symptoms other than a very high fever. In no time at all she was too weak to stand and suckle properly. The vet was totally mystified and told me that the only hope of keeping her alive was to see that she got enough fluid. This I did by milking her mother, adding a little water and glucose to the milk and feeding her at frequent intervals with a bottle. The combination of a good vet, a remarkable natural mother who, though normally a very highly strung donkey, allowed me to milk her and seemed to fully understand what I was doing for her baby and co-operated to the full, my devoted nursing and Debbie's own tenacity to life pulled her through. After a few days she was able to stand on tottery legs with some support and slowly suck from a patient mother who stood in exactly the right position with one leg back.

8

I feel that these early days when Debbie was kept alive not only by her mother but by me with the bottle, forged some sort of bond, almost like a mother/child relationship between us, or at least gave me a greater understanding of Debbie and certainly a special affection for her. Over the years I had so many instances of this direct mind-to-mind communication with Debbie. They were all quite simple things, a sudden clear picture in my mind of an empty water-trough in her paddock for instance.

Debbie was a great pet and over the years there were also innumerable instances when she appeared to have 'read' other people's minds. One occasion was when she was at Riding for The Disabled. A boy who had been detailed to lead her apparently felt that to lead a donkey was beneath his dignity and kept making derogatory comments about donkeys, and their lack of brain and beauty compared to horses. Debbie, while taking her usual customary care of the children managed to tread on his toe hard - twice - during the short time he was leading her. As she was then 9 years old and had never trodden on anyone's toe in her life before, it seemed rather beyond the bounds of coincidence that she should do it twice in the space of one short hour!

On another occasion I had a visitor to the stud looking at the donkeys. With her two young children she was standing by Debbie in the paddock and my hand was actually resting on Debbie's neck. My visitor, who had lived in Pakistan for twelve years, was telling me how the donkeys worked there, "They carry such big loads" she said "that you can only see the tips of their ears and their feet!". As she spoke, I felt Debbie's neck stiffen beneath my hand and with a reproachful look at the visitor, she walked firmly away. Her reaction was so obvious that the young woman laughed. "Oh dear - I have said the wrong thing mentioning work!" she said.

She had been telling her story well and had certainly put into my mind a clear picture of an over-laden donkey. Had such a picture been in her own mind to be picked it up by Debbie - or had she picked up from me? I do not know, but I am quite sure that Debbie too had a picture in her mind of an overloaded donkey and thought this was the moment to terminate the conversation!

I think probably the explanation, or partial explanation, for people who are very successful animal trainers is that they have this ability to see in their own mind very clear pictures and this is transmitted to the animal. A simple and quite common example of this is the successful rider/horse team in show-jumping. The successful show-jumping rider 'sees' the horse landing on the other side of the jump, the horse gets the picture and responds by jumping well.

Henry Flake, an Englishman, has written at length on communication between Man & Horse and Horse & Horse in his two books, 'Talking with Horses' & 'Thinking with Horses' published in England by Souvenir Press. He firmly believes that a great deal of communication between horses is by this transfer of mental pictures and says, in 'Talking With Horses' - 'Modern man appears almost completely to have lost the ability to transmit mental pictures, probably because this was the first skill he ceased to use when he gained the ability to speak. If you could describe with your voice what you were seeing, you did not need to transfer a mental picture'.

He and his wife did many experiments with horses, proving thought transference both from one horse to another and from man to horse and vice versa.

He writes how, with his favourite horse Weeping Roger, he could steer him to right and left, straight ahead or stop merely by thinking what he wanted him to do. On another occasion this facility for communication with the horse worked the other way, he woke suddenly in the middle of the night convinced that something was badly wrong with the horse; hurried down to the stables and found him in the grip of a bad attack of colic which would almost certainly have killed him without attention.

I have had very similar experiences with my own little mule, Pepita, who I have had for well over 20 years. There is a very close bond of affection between us and there have been many occasions when she definitely seems to have read my thoughts. I was out riding with my daughter one day and remarked in a conversational voice, "We'll turn back when we come to the next bend in the track". (We were riding through the bush at the time), at the next bend Pepita turned round without any instruction from me. I know that as I spoke I had a clear picture in my mind of the place I intended to turn for home. Quite often, too, she seemed to 'know' when I wanted to ride her.

She is very clever at crawling through wire fences and unless incarcerated in a paddock with an electric fence virtually had the run of the whole property. (She knew where home begins and ended however and never went through the boundary fences!). One morning my younger son asked me if I would ride with him, "Yes! - I replied, if you will find Pepita for me, I don't know where she is". I was amazed when he returned to the house only a few minutes later to tell me she was in the stable.

"I met her just coming up to the stables when I went out". He told me. "She must have known you wanted her". This sort of thing happened so often with her that I no longer dismiss it as coincidence.

One winter the clasp on her rug broke and I fastened it with a piece of string as a temporary repair. Each morning I would find the string undone and her rug skipping off. I couldn't

11

understand this, as, though she is very clever at undoing knots, it was a difficult (if not impossible) place for her to get at and I was sure anyway that she would not willingly undo her cosy rug and let in the cold and wet! One day as I adjusted it for the umpteenth time I said to her "However is this getting undone all the time, Pepita? She nuzzled me with her soft muzzle and simultaneously into my mind came a clear picture of Fleur, the pony filly who shared her paddock, picking the knot undone with her teeth. How incredibly stupid I had been not to think of this before, of course that was how it was getting undone! I decided to observe Fleur very carefully, preferably without her knowing it. Sure enough, a few days later, I saw her picking at the knot, exactly as I had already been 'told' she did by Pepita!

Pepita has the most beautiful eyes which have been referred to more than once by her admirers as 'speaking eyes'. Certainly they are to me, I feel that after years of close companionship with her I can tell almost everything she is thinking by the expression in her eyes. As one friend of mine often remarks, "I never knew an animal send out so many vibes' as Pepita!"

Indeed she does, and when they are vibes of dislike for someone I often find it quite embarrassing as it seems to me that she is making her feelings so obvious!

I am sure that with practice we can develop, or re-learn, the ability to 'see' in pictures and thus transmit messages to our animal friends, and receive them too, of course. It was when I received a message from one of my dogs that I decided to try an experiment in transmitting to Cindy.

My husband had been shopping at the supermarket one day and was unloading the goods in the kitchen, watched as always by an interested trio of dogs. As he put the tins of dog meat down Cindy looked at them, then glanced at me. As she did so I got a clear mental picture, exactly like a colour slide, of the tin of meat. Without thinking I remarked to my husband.

"Oh good, Cindy says that's her favourite meat!" He looked at me in some surprise. "How do you mean 'she says'. How did I know? I suppose because she had just told me.

I decided to see if I could get my thoughts over to her. It had to be something simple with an obvious answer. I consciously made a mental picture of Cindy sitting down, trying to put the 'picture' on a white screen in my mind, just like a colour slide in fact. Within a few seconds Cindy sat down, I have done this countless times and providing I could get the picture clear enough in my own mind Cindy received it and duly sat down without any verbal or outward sign from me. This is a very simple experiment that anyone can try out with their own dog.

The closer one is to an animal, the more one can both receive and transmit from it, you are more likely to be tuned in, or on the same wavelength as we say. Each autumn either I or my husband, or both of us 'get the message' from Pepita that she feels it is time to start wearing her rug. My husband and I have often discussed this, we don't really know how, that is in what form, we receive the message. We only know that somehow around the end of May, we do. My husband will come in one day and say - "Pepita feels it's time she has her rug on". Or I will say to him "I'd better get Pepita's rug out, she says it is about time she had it on". Neither of us feels there is anything in the least odd about these remarks, because we know that we are getting that message!

Having a lot of different animals around the place can provide a great deal of interest to the animal lover in observing their relationships with one another and the way they obviously communicate.

Two of our dogs loved to go off on rabbiting expeditions together. Something that was definitely not encouraged. Minnie, the little Foxie, could get stuck down a rabbit hole, and Cindy, fox size and colour could be mistaken for a fox and shot. Also if off our own property and on neighbouring paddocks among sheep, their motives could have been misconstrued and they could both be shot. We tried whenever possible, never to have them both outside the house together without adequate supervision. Even so they managed many expeditions. A keen observer could see them communicating, sometimes 'sniffing noses', sometimes with eye contact, then bat your eyes - turn your head half a turn away, take all your concentration off them for a second and they were gone.

Watching a paddock of cows and calves I noticed that one cow appeared to be in charge of a large group of calves lying around dozing while their mothers graze a distance away. I wondered if they have a roster worked out, whether they take it in a definite turns to 'baby-sit' or whether one particularly obliging and maternal cow did most of it?

Times without number I have seen donkey mothers 'telling' their foals what to do; quite soundlessly, merely by looking. One particularly dramatic occasion occurred with a little jenny we had, called 'Misty'. She had been staying at a stud near Broadford to be served by an imported English donkey stallion. She had a foal at foot. When we went to fetch her home she was running in a large paddock of 100 acres or so with the stallion and a small group of jennies. When we went to catch them the first reaction of the jennies, including Misty, was to trot away. They were quite close to us and were not doing this with any very serious intent. Misty suddenly stopped dead, looked round at her foal, looked him steadily in the eye for a second, then jumped what at first I took to be a branch or a piece of bark. When it began to move I saw it was a large brown snake. Misty's foal, just behind her, copied her exactly and jumped neatly over the snake. Both of course were quite unharmed. Not so Benjamin, the English donkey. Brought up far from the hot dry paddocks and venomous snakes of Australia he blundered on, treading on the tail of the snake, which promptly reared up and bit him on the shoulder. Thanks to the prompt attention of a good vet, who came at once when summoned and accompanied by a police escort with sirens blaring, the story ended happily. Misty's behaviour was a most interesting example of communication between animals. She obviously communicated in that penetrating look to her foal that there was danger - but not to panic, just be careful and do as she did.

Another rather amusing example of animal communication and co-operation occurred one day with Debbie, this time between her and her real-life donkey mother, Dinah. Debbie and Dinah were having their breakfast in the yard together out of a wooden box that was actually an old ammunition crate and was approximately the length of a sheep. Betsy, my daughter's very fat and greedy pet sheep was also eating their breakfast and to do it was standing lengthwise in the trough, thus making it almost impossible for Debbie and Dinah to get anything. First Dinah turned round and kicked Betsy, then Debbie did the same. Unperturbed Betsy went on eating. Dinah and Debbie looked at one another over her woolly back, then they both turned round and kicked her at the same time. This was too much for Betsy, with a grunt of disgust, she lumbered out of the trough. The message that had passed between the two donkeys was obviously something along these lines - "Well - we don't seem to be doing much good - let's try it at the same time - come on - NOW!"

Animals not only can communicate with us but can show an extraordinary understanding of circumstances, if we are only open to receive what they are transmitting.

Many years ago, when I was a very small child, we had a tiny cross-bred Yorkshire terrier dog. Mickey was not as big as a fair-sized cat, but one of the most intelligent, toughest and bravest little characters I have ever known. He was a fantastic ratter and an intrepid fighter, prepared to take on any dog - no matter how large. He was also a very good little watchdog, barking with his shrill yap, loud and long at any untoward sound or stranger.

One night my father was away from home and the only occupants of our large country farmhouse was my mother, the resident maid (this was in pre-war days!), myself and my baby brother. About two in the morning my mother was wakened by Mickey, but not by him barking downstairs in the kitchen, but by him standing by her on the bed, gently tapping her face and whining very softly. Astonished at such unusual behaviour, she got up and, putting on her dressing gown, followed him quietly downstairs without putting any lights on. It was a bright moonlit night for one thing, but more important, she was getting the message, from the normally noisy little dog, for the need for silence.

Together they crept down the stairs, at the foot of the stairs, she could see the glass panel of the side door, and silhouetted through it in the moonlight, the figure of a man. For a moment, in her own words, she froze - almost cried out - then silently she and Mickey crept back upstairs.

My father, when he came home, was most impressed by Mickey's behaviour. Had he barked, as he normally did, he would certainly have betrayed the fact that in this lonely farmhouse there were no-one but women, children and a brave, but very small and not really formidable, little dog. But by going quietly upstairs and waking my mother he had alerted her to the possibility of danger without giving anything away.

My mother, when talking of this incident afterwards, often referred to the real communication and understanding that flowed then between her and the dog, as much, or more than if they were actually talking out loud to each other.

These moments when we can communicate without words with animals most often seem to come without conscious effort. My mother wakened from sleep, would be in a relaxed, perhaps almost dream-like, frame of mind, a perfect condition to receive messages from another mind.

An interesting point about this mind-to-mind communication which exists, not only between animals but now and then between animals and people, is that these people who have experienced a near-death experience, or who have clinically died and been brought back to life, or those who have in some way or another had an out of body experience, almost invariably talk about this direct and instantaneous communication between people in the spirit world, with no language barriers or, in fact, need for language or words.

This poses food for thought. Is the acquiring of the sophisticated oral communication skills which mankind has developed an advance or not? Have we to some extent lost a greater skill? Are the animals in fact, not less, but more advanced than us?

There is of course one remarkable animal, that has developed communication skills to a very high level, and that is the dolphin.

These remarkable creatures have a brain that is relatively larger than that of Man. Comparing the two brains, that of man and that of the dolphin, Dr. Horace Dobbs, scientist, conservationist, film-maker, but above all, world famous expert on dolphins, says; "Our brain has moved into a kind of situation where it is like a computer and, I'm not sure the dolphin's brain is like a computer. I think it is in tune with natural vibrations. It may well be taking in other signals which we may not be sensitive to, or we've got a reduced sensitivity to." He goes on to talk about how they suffer from sensory deprivation in captivity, adding that even when free in the sea they are being threatened by Man's pollution of the environment, particularly by Sonic pollution. "We don't know how much interference we are doing but it could be like you and I trying to communicate with a pneumatic drill going on. Fish finders on ships operate right in the middle of a dolphin's frequency communication band".

Study of dolphins has revealed that they do indeed communicate extremely well with one another in a language composed of sonic and supersonic 'squeaks'. What is even more amazing is that they can 'imitate' human speech, but at a much faster rate. This was accidentally discovered by Dr. John Lilly, a neurophysiologist who was studying the swimming skills of dolphins, in order to develop a better and more efficient submarine for the U.S. Navy. When a tape of dolphin voices was played back at a speed eight times lower then normal, it was found to be a reproduction of human speech!

Dr. Lilly has written a book called 'Man & Dolphin' in which he also related numerous incidents of dolphins altruistically helping one another when in danger, and even helping human beings.

Without exception the scientists and others who have studied the dolphin have been amazed and impressed by their sophisticated communication skills and many have expressed the view that if only we could learn to listen and rid ourselves of the notion that we are in every way superior, we could expand immeasurably the horizons of our knowledge.

Man, in fact, is not nearly as clever at learning the language of animals as they are at learning the meaning, even if they cannot reproduce the sounds, of human speech.

There is the case of the chimpanzee in America who learned some 200 or so words in Deaf & Dumb language, and what is more, learned to put them together, in simple phrases and short sentences. There are also the many documented cases of animals being taught to talk by a series of tapes etc, to indicate letters and thus have communicated by a painstaking tapping out of letters, forming words and even sentences in a sort of morse code.

One such 'experiment' is recorded in a book called 'The Talking Dogs' by Maurice Rowdon. The two dogs, were Elke, a Standard Poodle female, and Belam, a Saluki male. The dogs lived in Bavaria with their owner Frau Heilemaier (Mami), but were taught by their resident teacher, Fraulein Dorothy Meyer. Between March 1974 and the end of 1975 they had approximately 500, lessons, each one of which was painstakingly 'logged' (mistakes included) by Dorothy. To this she added approximately 40 hours of taped impressions of the dogs and their work and it is this material that forms the basis of Maurice Rowdon's book.

What emerges is not only the astonishing discovery that the dogs did actually learn to communicate and could recognise things drawn or written on a blackboard but much of their thoughts and opinions of the human beings who were so important in their lives and also the undeniable fact that they understood a great deal more of what was going on and human conversation that dogs are usually given credit for!

I am convinced of the truth of this, and it is a salutary thought! By my own observations of the animals who share our family life. I remember one day my husband and I were freezing sweet corn in the kitchen, 'Heidi', our German Shepherd, who loves nothing better than a ride in the car, was lying in the hall, out of sight but within earshot. I had to go shopping and I said to my husband, in a conversational voice, "I'll do the rest when I come back." The wording here is particularly important, because I did not use any 'key' words that Heidi could be said to recognise, such as 'car', 'shopping', or even 'I'm going now'. But I had barely spoken before Heidi was in the kitchen, looking at me expectantly, tail wagging, as she always did when a trip in the car was in the offing.

Most of the time we are not observing our animals really closely when we are talking to other members of the family. Try a little experiment, for one whole day at least, longer if possible, watch your dog carefully when you are talking to other people. I guarantee you will be surprised how often he betrays by a look or an action that he does know what you are taking about!

There are other forms of communication between ourselves and our animal friends which we either dismiss as nonsense or push to the back of our minds as something we would rather not think about - too exotic - too spiritual - too - way out.

One of these is aura. All living things emanate an aura. Kirlian photography has proved this beyond doubt. Many gifted psychics can actually see this aura without the benefit of photography, so can animals.

This explains to a great extent why animals so often immed-iately like, or dislike, a person. Animal lovers have an orange glow in their aura which is seen and recognised by animals. Fear, on the other hand gives a turgid brown look to the aura, this stimulates a reciprocal fear in the animal together with anger and a desire to attack.

Dogs, we often say, can 'smell fear'. Science has now proved that this is much more than an idle saying. Fear accelerates many of the bodily functions making people 'sweat with fear' to a greater or lesser extent; this has a distinctive smell which undoubtedly is smelt by animals.

Some humans claim to be very sensitive to 'atmosphere', such as knowing when there is tension between two people who have recently been quarrelling, even though the quarrel took place before they came into the room or even into the building.

In actual fact what they have is probably a very good sense of smell and what they are doing is smelling the pheromones which are chemical substances emitted by various creatures in states of excitement or tension, such as quarrelling violently. Thus these people can smell fear or anger in exactly the same way that a dog does.

There is a form of communication between Man and Animal when a Spiritual or Psychic healer treats an animal. Animals, unlike humans, almost invariably show their appreciation of this form of healing, to do this they must be receiving some form of 'communication' if only in the sense of well-being they feel.

Sylvia Broadwood, a medium and healer who, with the help of the Spiritualist Association of Great Britain has a Healing Clinic for animals in Central London, said that animals invariably show their gratitude and never forget. 'Human love is a necessity to animals in their development. We should make an effort to talk to our pets. They do understand and can help us as well as themselves."

Love of course is the key that opens doors and the instrument that breaks barriers. It is not mere chance that those animals and people who make the greatest headway in communication between Man and the Animal world are those who love and are loved in return.

Chapter Two

The Healers

Many people confuse Psychic, or Spiritual healing with Faith healing and because of this, wonder how it is possible for an animal to be healed. Animals, they reason, cannot have the sort of unreserved blind faith in the healer that cures.

Psychic or Spiritual healing however does not need faith, or indeed anything, on the part of the person or animal being healed. In fact it can even be done without their knowledge.

However to understand better we must clarify just what healing is. All healing, ultimately, comes from within, from ourselves. Whether we are treated by conventional methods or by a psychic healer it is our own inner powers, both of body and mind, that will ultimately heal us.

We know that if we are run-down, tired or at a physical low ebb in some way we are much more likely to succumb to colds, influenza or any other 'bug' that is around. Undernourished children or animals are likely to become sickly and are prey to any ailment that comes along.

Similarly on a psychic or spiritual level, when our batteries are low we suffer a loss of power - to help ourselves or others. Jesus - the greatest healer of all time - knew all about this, Invariably when healing he told people to "Go - fast and pray". In other words, rest the body and raise the mind to a higher level thus giving both a chance to re-charge the batteries.

Even more explicitly when a woman touched the hem of his garment, he 'felt it' and asked who touched him, saying "I felt the power leave me".

Brought down to its basics, this is what healing is. An exchange of power. We all, every living creature, have this power, it is the life force running through us and can be felt at times like an electrical charge.

Try this simple experiment: Put your two hands in front of you, palms facing in a typical praying gesture but do not let them actually touch, keep a space half to a quarter of an inch between the palms, relax as completely as possible, but concentrate your attention on your hands. Imagining, if you like, that you have a soft ball, a piece of plasticine, a lump of bread dough, anything that is soft and pliable between your hands, move your hands slightly as if rolling this object between the two palms and this will probably be followed by a tingling of the fingers.

We all have healing powers, but in some it is stronger than in others. These people will sometimes receive such a strong sensation that it is almost like a mild electric shock, they may even notice small red patches or blotches on the palms of the hands.

It is this power, this personal electricity if you will, that is transmitted from the healer to the healed. If you pass your hand very slowly backwards and forwards over the part of the body of the animal or person you wish to heal you will probably feel a change of temperature, often a patch of what seems to be colder air, just over the spot and your patient will probably tell you that they can feel a pleasant feeling of warmth when your hand is just over the area. It is not necessary to actually touch the skin, just pass the hand about a centimetre above the surface.

Your animal patients of course will not be able to tell you in so many words just what they are feeling but if you observe them carefully you will usually notice a definite relaxation in their attitude. Cats will often show their appreciation by purring, a dog may wag his tail or turn and lick your hand.

Healing of this sort can often be a great help to the animal in addition to orthodox veterinary treatment. When Cindy, one of my dogs, had stitches in a nasty gash on her side the wound healed amazingly quickly with the aid of two or three sessions daily of a few minutes each and she herself obviously felt a definite benefit for she would position herself for me to do it and as my hands passed above the injury she would wag her tail.

This form of direct healing or exchange of power with animals is however a two way thing.

Who among us has not felt better when coming home tired and perhaps with raw and jangled nerves after 'one of those days' when a beloved dog has put his head on our knee to be stroked, a favourite cat jumped onto our lap with a soft purr of greeting. As we reach out a hand, ostensibly to caress, we feel ourselves relax and know that we are receiving more than we are giving.

This is indeed so much more than idle speculation or mere wishful thinking. A study of patients who have undergone serious heart surgery has shown that those who go home to pets have a considerably higher survival rate than those who do not.

People who habitually sit with a cat on their lap or who sleep with a cat on the bed are said to suffer less from all forms of rheumatism due to the amount of static electricity in the cat's coat. Whether this is so I do not know as no serious research seems to have been done on the subject, certainly the cat herself is one domestic animal who never suffers from rheumatism. Dogs, cattle and especially horses can all get very stiff and suffer from rheumatism and/or arthritis as they age.

Cats, in fact seem to have gained a considerable mastery over old age. They show very few of the signs of advancing years compared with Man and other animals. They remain astonishingly agile, if a little less active, they do not go grey and their hearing and eyesight shows little sign of impairment even into quite advanced old age.

Anyone who has kept many cats or had much to do with them as pets will surely at some time or other have had the sensations of receiving a mild electric shock when stroking their pet, even perhaps of actually seeing sparks. I remember returning home from an evening out one cool, crisp evening. As I stepped out of the car and reached for the switch on the wall to put on the outside light, one of my cats trotted up mewing a greeting. I bent down to stroke him and was astonished to note not only a faint tingling in my fingers but to actually see a distinct shower of sparks. No wonder the humble domestic cat was capable of striking such fear into the minds and hearts of simple souls in the superstitious Middle Ages!

Evidence of the two way effects of this healing power came to me quite unexpectedly. I was sitting relaxed in my favourite armchair with my white cat, Sheba, curled on my lap. With the tips of my fingers I was just passing over the patches of excema which recurred with her from time to time hoping that some healing influence would flow from my fingers to her. On the thumb of my right hand I had a band-aid over a small, but quite painful, little cut that had been self-inflicted by my careless handling of a kitchen knife when preparing vegetables. As my hand passed over Sheba's body I felt a warm glow in this thumb accompanied by a pulsing, rather than a throbbing, not in any way a painful sensation. When I removed the band-aid some time later with a view to replacing it with a fresh one I was amazed to see the small cut had completely healed.

In today's technological world with its passion for specialisation there is a strict dividing line between those who doctor people and those who doctor animals.

It has not always been so. Up to comparatively recent times, the herbalist treated man and beast alike and the bone-setter set broken bones whether in two-legged or four-legged patients.

Dr. Axel Munthe who was renowned throughout Europe as a physician and had the wealthy and the famous flocking to his fashionable consulting rooms when he practiced in Paris and later in Rome, says in his autobiographical book, 'The Story of San Michele', that at one time he had almost more dog patients than human ones!

He was also called in professionally to treat many of the animals, particularly the primates, at the Paris zoo. This was not so very long ago for Dr. Munthe only died in 1948.

Many Psychic healers treat both animals and humans. Gordon Turner, one of the great English healers and for many years editor of the magazine 'Global Light' which dealt with Spiritualism and healing, both of animals and people, wrote in his book 'An Outline of Spiritual Healing' - 'Healing power is not restricted to any one life form. The same healing that will ease the arthritis in the legs of a human patient will just as readily ease the pain of an animal. All life is part of the Supreme Spirit. There is not one healing for animals and another for people. We have the same God and we react to the same power of love'.

Gordon Turner held separate clinics for animals and people at one time, then he decided that this was unnecessary and he held one clinic for both animal and human patients. He adds that he had no complaints from his human patients, that the animals did not quarrel between themselves and that in fact their manners were impeccable.

In common with other healers who treat animals he says how appreciative they were of the treatment, in fact so much so that he sometimes could not get rid of them as patients! A cat that he had been treating for a tumour turned up on her own two successive weeks after the owner had been told that she needed no further treatment. She was only stopped attending the clinic by herself by being shut up on that evening to prevent her setting off across the town and crossing busy streets, with all it's dangers, by herself!

He also found that animals were, if anything, even more responsive to absent healing than people. This I can attest to as many years ago my own beloved little white cat. Tiny, had a tumour which disappeared when he treated her by absent healing. This was in the days when he was editing 'Global Light' and I was contributing articles on animals. I told him about Tiny's tumour and he offered to heal her. I was then living in the English Midlands and he was in London.

He has some delightful stories to tell about his animal patients, among them the one about the little black and white mongrel bitch who was not really a patient at all. She was brought to him by her owner one evening. Gordon knelt down and examined her carefully all over but could find no sign of anything wrong with her at all. When he asked her owner what was the matter he was told, "Nothing, but I read in the paper that dogs never bite you; as she bites everyone else I thought I would see if it was true!"

In fact he says in his book, that in all the years that he had treated all sorts of animals he has never been bitten, kicked, scratched or molested in any way.

He found that birds reacted particularly well to Spiritual healing, and that even wild birds would lie quietly in the palm of his hand during healing.

"I believe, he wrote," that animals have a life after death - just as we do - and that they pass through stages of spiritual evolution and change. I look forward to the day when animal healing will be a normal part of the practice of every healer and I feel sure that this will help to contribute to a truer perspective in understanding the place which animals occupy in the scheme of being. And that one day the sanctity of all life may be observed as a basic principle by the whole of mankind".

Another great healer, Dr. Albert Schweitzer said much the same thing when he wrote; "Compassion, in which all ethics must take root, can only attain it's full breadth and depth if it embraces all living creatures and does not limit itself to Mankind".

Many people tend to see spiritual healing as something set apart, even in some way contrary to, orthodox healing. In this they are quite wrong and throughout the ages the greatest doctors have been those who are also healers, whether they knew it or not.

We all use healing in our everyday lives. When we stroke a sick animal or caress a sick child we are using healing, we are offering in fact some of our own power to that animal or person. When our thoughts go out in sympathy and concern for someone we love who is distant from us and sick we are practicing absent healing. When we pray for the sick we are practicing exactly the same thing. When our prayers are answered we make the mistake of thinking that our appeal to God has been heard and that alone is what has helped the sick person; the truth is both deeper and simpler. We have sent out love and healing. By our prayers we have added to the power because we in our turn have also drawn on a source of divine power.

A remarkable story of absent healing in which animals were involved in a strange way was reported in the newspaper, *Psychic News* in Sept. 1955.

The subject was a woman who was a school teacher and also an animal welfare worker in the Far East. She was suffering from an advanced cancer and was due to go into hospital on Monday August 1st to be operated on the following day.

Early on the Sunday morning, the day before she was due to go into hospital, she had a very strange and clear dream. In her dream she found herself in a beautiful field separated from another similar field by a river spanned by a bridge. In the other field were a group of people, all of whom she recognised as her own dead loved ones. Her mother, grandfather, aunt and several friends.

They all seemed very happy, and called to her, smiling and waving, obviously expecting her to join them. Though she knew quite well they were dead, she was not in the least afraid for they all seemed so happy and natural. She stepped onto the bridge to join them.

Half-way across the bridge she was met by a whole bevy of dogs rushing to meet her, obviously over-joyed to see her. Again she recognised all the dogs as those she had known and who had died. Some had shared her home as special friends, others had lived in the home she had founded for them. When she had spoken to them all and fondled them, she tried to continue her way over the bridge. But the dogs barred her way. She remonstrated with them and tried to move them aside or get through them but without success.

Then she realised there was a man dressed in a loose robe at her side. She appealed to him for help to reach the other side. But he told her; "You cannot cross this bridge". "But I must!" she insisted. "My mother is over there, I want to talk to her!"

"You cannot cross this bridge." He repeated. Then with a sweep of his arm he indicated another road - a long way round. "But there is another way, though it is a very long road."

Obediently she began to walk backwards off the bridge, away from the people on the other side. The dogs came with her until she was back where she started then they turned and went back to their side of the river.

As she began to take the road indicated by the man she woke up. The following day she presented herself at the hospital where she was examined again, this time by another specialist, a surgeon. To her amazement, and incredulous belief, he could find no sign of cancer.

A remarkable footnote to this story is that subsequent enquiries revealed that she was dreaming this remarkable dream at the very time that healing was being asked for her. The healing also appeared to be complete as some years later she still had no signs of cancer.

The part of the dogs in the dream is very important, highlighting many points. First of course the fact that they were there, just as much as her human loved ones. Then there is the two-way aspect; just as we can help our animal friends, so it seems, can they help us. Finally we have the connecting link, the thread that runs through the whole amazing little story, which is, of course love. Both the love between human souls on two planes of existence and the love between animals and human, human and animals on both the physical and the astral planes.

Gordon Turner refers to the healing power as the 'energy of love' and in a delightful story about a small black kitten he relates how he learned, from this same kitten, that there is no limit to this power.

He was woken early one morning by someone in a car begging him to come with them to treat a kitten that had been run over. Dressing hurriedly he accompanied them to a flat in North London. When he got there a vet had also been called and had already given the kitten an injection to end it's sufferings. It lay on the floor, a pathetic black scrap, to all intents and purposes, dead.

"Obviously there was nothing I could do, but seeing the owner's terrible distress I suggested that we should kneel together by the kitten with our hands just above him and pray for the easy passing of its spirit to a happier land".

They knelt like that for two or three minutes, then, he says, "I felt a strange sensation under my hands. It was just as if fur was being rubbed against the palms. I looked down and saw to my amazement, that it had lifted itself to it's feet and was rubbing it's back against my hands."

It soon began to purr, and then walked across the room and drank some milk from its bowl, and lived to maturity and a normal cat-life!

The theme that all life is one, that we give help and we receive help is stressed by all great healers and gradually, it seems, we are coming to accept that we can receive power and help from our animal friends. In fact 'Pet Therapy' is being used more by the medical profession, who, it seems have just discovered what animal-lovers have known for a long time. That pets are good for you!

In Melbourne, a Golden Labrador called Honey was recently the subject of a television program. Honey has been added to the staff of an old people's ward in a Melbourne Hospital and proved a resounding success in her job. Not only a focal point of interest, but a living, loving, totally un-critical friendly personality, she has given a whole new dimension to the patient's lives. The only problem encountered so far has been Honey's rapidly expanding waist-line due to her habit of scrounging endless snacks and bickies!

Studies of pets and people have revealed among other things, increased life-span in heart-attach victims, lowering of blood-pressure and marked progress in mentally retarded children.

Joan Goodricke working with seriously handicapped, both physically and mentally, children in Hobart used donkeys for some years in her work. The mentally retarded she found relate to the animals in a way that they cannot to people and the physically handicapped can enjoy their company, for donkeys are extremely gentle.

There is a thriving 'Driving for The Disabled' movement in England that also uses donkeys extensively, again because of their calm and gentle temperaments.

The Slade Centre in England runs a unique venture in co-operation with the Donkey Sanctuary. Here donkeys who themselves were rescued have been trained to be ridden and driven by handicapped children. The centre was started in 1978 thanks to the imagination and hard work of Mrs. Elizabeth Svensdon who runs the Sanctuary. The idea of using some of these rescued donkeys – at one time she had 250 in her care – came to her as an inspirational flash at 3 am one morning in 1975 and she organised a trial session.

The results were amazing, it was obvious that there was a great bond between the donkeys and the children from the very start. Autistic children began to relate, Hyper-active children quietened and even spastic and severely handicapped children made physical movements previously thought impossible by Doctors, Therapists and teachers.

Following the success of the trial session Elizabeth Svensdon, with the help of her husband and four carefully selected trustees which included the headmaster of a handicapped school and representatives from the school services and the Medical and Teaching profession, formed a registered charity. They drew up careful plans for a purpose-built centre and set about obtaining planning permission and raising the necessary finance.

The centre finally opened in December 1978 with a large arena for riding indoors, a field for summer riding, a track where donkeys pull sulkies, stables where donkeys can be petted, tack and feed room and a special mounting block for the severely disabled. In addition to this there is a viewing gallery and a special observation room where visiting educational and medical staff can watch through one way glass and from which heating, ventilation, the loudspeaker system and a special sprinkler system to keep down dust, can be operated.

Between the inception of the idea and the opening of the centre, Mrs. Svensden and her helpers took the donkeys to handicapped schools within a 20 mile radius who were prepared to fully co-operate in the scheme and keep careful records of progress etc, thus the scheme was adequately tested before the actual opening of the centre. The following extract from a letter from the head teacher of the most severely handicapped school visited, is self-explanatory.

"...We must admit that the first Thursday you came it was all great fun for the children, but we honestly thought that you and your helpers were living in cloud cuckoo land, with your records of progress and mounting and sitting and other things you asked us to do. All the staff wish me to tell you how very wrong we were - the progress of so many children has really amazed us - the different way they now sit and how so many of them can now sit without support. Tim who is so spastic has now got the idea of sitting up. The joy the rides bring to the blind, very sub-normal James. The real laughter that came from those who very seldom laugh. Perhaps the greatest thing to us is the motivation it has given to Stephen - for three years we have tried to find something to motivate this very withdrawn little boy who lives in a world of his own - the first day we saw him climb on the donkeys - on his own - well we could have cried. I don't think you and your great band of helpers quite realise the good you have done to these severely sub-normal, multiply handicapped children.."

The aims and objectives of the scheme are not to merely give handicapped children riding skills but to give them the chance to love, pet and cuddle the donkeys, in itself therapeutic.

Donkeys would appear to be particularly successful in this sort of work, they are cuddly, extremely affectionate and they seem to have a built-in regard for children. In spite of the fact that they are pushy and friendly they are also extremely gentle.

Norah Russell, at one time the owner of a large donkey stud near Melbourne told me how her grandson who was physically handicapped with his legs in callipers, could go out in the paddock with some dozen or so jenny donkeys and never come to any harm as they crowded round him, even though he would have lost his balance with a slight push. Female donkeys are extremely good mothers and I think they often extend this maternal, caring, instinct to human children.

The University of Pennsylvania recently held a conference on the human/animal companion bond that attracted some 500 interested people from both sides of the fence, so to speak. Anthropologists and animal behaviourists, veterinarians and psychiatrists all anxious to study the importance of pet animals in relation to human health.

In Washington the Arlington Animal Welfare League runs what it calls a 'pet-therapy programme' in which it takes animals for visits to homes in the area.

Martha Armstrong, the executive director, said it began almost by chance. When she found herself unable to get home for Christmas she and two of her staff members went along to visit the inmates of a local nursing home taking along a few of the animals from the shelter. The visit was such a success that they gained permission to make such visits regularly, then other Homes in the area heard about it and also asked if they could have animal visitors.

A similar scheme was started by Dr Leo Bustad of Washington State University's Veterinary school. When his mother was sick he smuggled her dog in to visit her in the hospital. The reaction from the other patients was so great, all wanting to touch the dog, 'as if they were starving for something', he said, that he thought up 'Bustad's People-pet Partnership Programme' and in 1975 the first animal, a cat, was 'placed' in a nursing home.

"The beauty of animals" says Dr. Bustad, "Is that they make no judgments. They are always accepting and they don't care how you look."

Sylvia Broadwood, a renowned English healer, has a special healing clinic for animals in Central London. She says that her patients never fail to express their gratitude and thanks to her, not only for their own healing but often for that of their owners as well.

In proof of this she tells the story of the little terrier that 'appeared' and rested his paws on her lap. Clever with a pencil, Sylvia did a sketch of him. Later when this was shown to a woman she had healed she identified it at once as a faithful likeness of a dearly loved dog who had died 35 years previously. This as Sylvia pointed out - is also proof that our dead pets are not dead but still walk with us.

Sylvia's healing gift with her animal patients is enhanced by her great empathy with them enabling her in so many instances to understand how they are feeling and what is really troubling them.

"Love" she explains, is the key to her success. "For human love is necessary to these animals which we have made so dependent on us for their happiness and development."

"We should all" - she says - "Make an effort to talk to our pets. They do understand and can help us as well as themselves."

Chapter Three

Animals and Christianity

'The cat has caught a bird - the wicked cat must die. And she resumed her quail on toast and he his pigeon pie.'

The above couplet encapsulates for me the double standard of both the Christian ethic and individual Christians when it comes to attitudes towards and dealings with the animal kingdom.

In today's materialistic world where we have everything neatly documented and slotted into its correct compartment the Christian Church, for the most part, stands apart from concern for animals. We have the powerful 'Right to Life Movement' which stands for the right to life of human beings, but conveniently forgets that other creatures too have a right to life. How seldom today do we hear an ecclesiastical voice speaking bravely out against vivisection, bull-fighting or any of the other atrocities committed against the animal kingdom by Man?

There are of course a few notable exceptions, St Francis of Assissi, Albert Schweitzer and of course, Jesus himself; to name a few. How far has Christianity strayed from the message of St Francis and from Jesus?

What set these 'greats' apart was not merely that they were kind to animals but that they knew the oneness of life. That every living thing is of God and God is in every living thing.

They did not merely talk about the sacredness of all life - they lived it.

St Francis not only loved animals and preached to the birds and fishes, he took care not to walk on earth-worms and when he washed his hands he poured the water away where it could flow and not be trodden into mud. Albert Schweitzer would not even kill flies if he could help it.

Jesus said, "Look at the birds of the air, they do now sow or reap or gather into barns, yet your father feeds them." Making the point that God cares for birds just as he does for people. All are part of the same great family of living creatures dependent on the same life-giving source for their needs.

In today's world we are in danger of forgetting this most basic fact, a fact not merely of life - but of survival itself.

St Francis of Assissi is a 'popular' saint, and a very well-known one. Most of us have a picture in our minds of a kindly avuncular figure surrounded by animals and birds. When thinking of Christians and animals at the same time most people immediately think of St Francis. Many of them, alas, would either go along with Voltaire's view of him as a 'raving lunatic who went about stark naked talking to animals' or take a more kindly, but still rather patronising view of him - as Liam Brophy puts it in his poem, St Francis:

> The world may think him queer or quaint,
> A troubadour, a jolly saint
> Who babbled blithely to the birds
> In courteous, poetic words -
> A far-off figure, mauve and faint.

They do not listen to his message or see it as having any relevance to the world today - they do not even understand his message. His view of the world was one which needs to be understood and acted upon by whole nations if we are not to destroy ourselves and the rest of creation.

This is the belief held by Fr. Eric Doyle, an English Franciscan priest who feels so strongly about it that he has written a remarkable book called 'St Francis & The Song Of Brotherhood' in the hope that a more universal acceptance of the philosophy of St Francis might help to curse the evils of selfishness and consumerism that are in danger of bringing about the destruction of life as we know it, on this planet.

Francis did not see the world as something created for our pleasure and convenience, to be used and used up, as we see fit, but as a sort of giant jigsaw of physical, personal, spiritual and cosmic relationships in which humanity, along with all other created things fitted into place.

St Francis was not kind to animals simply because he liked them. He loved them, as part of the brotherhood of all life in God. To him God was in the hare, the lamb and the wolf that he talked to and instructed in the ways of Christian love. They were, in the truest sense, his brothers and sisters because we are all part of God's creation.

St Francis loved animals and he also loved his fellow men, be they saints, sinners or lepers. Eight centuries later Albert Schweitzer who was a doctor of theology as well as medicine and devoted his life to the service of his fellow men wrote: 'Compassion, in which all ethics must take root, can only attain its full breadth and depth if it embraces all living creatures and does not limit itself to mankind'.

Two Franciscan priests I spoke to while writing this book left me in doubt that, as far as animals and our relationship with them were concerned, their thinking was not quite in line with their founder, the saint who Paul Gallico called 'A man among saints'. I was interested to see if they were influenced by St Francis in their attitude towards the non-human animals who share this earth with us.

The first one, who I was told was considered something of an authority on St Francis told me that he thought St Francis went a little too far and that it wasn't necessary to be a vegetarian. All that was required was that we weren't actively cruel.

The second, a parish priest, admitted that he never thought about preaching kindness to animals from the pulpit or to children in school to whom he gave religious instruction, adding that he was far too busy dealing with young delinquents to bother about animals.

It did not seem to have crossed his mind that a more generally caring and all-embracing view of living creature, both human and non-humans in which both animals and the delinquents together in a loving interaction of relationships could help both. And if this was a way of life from earliest childhood there might not even be so many delinquents!

Given the opportunity to care for - and love - another living creature can sometimes have the most remarkable effect on those who have never known love themselves. This has been proved in America by the success of a bold experiment called 'The Last Chance Mule Train'.

In this experiment, hardened young offenders were 'sentenced' by the courts to travel across America along the old mule-train pioneering trails with a mule train, called 'The Last Chance' because that is exactly what it is - their last chance before being sentenced to a much harsher form of imprisonment. These young people, aged between fifteen and twenty, had all been through the courts - some several times – and were considered hardened cases.

The great majority of these young offenders had never had any close personal contact with any animal before, but they were assigned to a horse or mule and made responsible for its well-being on the trail. The results were spectacular. The numbers getting into trouble with the law after they had taken part in this, being far, far lower than after any other form of detention or punishment. The realisation that another living creature depended solely on them for care and comfort, that they were important to someone else, even if that some-one were 'only' a mule, was the breakthrough that was needed.

An interesting point, which probably has some psychological value, is that for many of the mules, the trek was also their last chance. They were outlaw mules destined to end up in a can or at the glue factory unless they too could be reformed. The great majority of them were. They were broken and trained during the course of the trail by the young delinquents and by journey's end, both were ready to take their place in the world.

Many sincere Christians tend to play down or belittle their love for animals because they are made to feel, by the teachings of the Church, that it is somehow un-important, or even worse, a defect in their character and the old chestnut is bandied around about 'people caring for animals instead of people'. No statement could be more patently absurd and a glance at the lives of the great saints of the Church proves this.

St Martin de Porres, the South American saint, born in Lima, in Peru, in 1579, the son of a Spanish Knight and a negro woman, entered the Dominican Order at the age of 15 as a lay brother and became a great benefactor of the poor and the weak and helpless; a caring that he extended to animals as well as people and, with the help of his sister, founded what was virtually a sanctuary for sick and stray animals.

His understanding and rapport with all animals was so great that when the monastery was invaded by rats he talked to them and persuaded them to leave and collect in a barn where he promised to feed them. There is also the well known story of how he persuaded a cat, dog, rat and bird all to eat as brothers from the same dish.

That this is truth and not just a charming fairy story is borne out by Hereward Carrington in his book *"Your Psychic Powers and How to Develop Them"* when he says, writing about the attainment of a higher spiritual level, "You will find that you exert a peculiar influence over all animals with whom you come into contact, and that they not only know and understand you, but, if the animals are wild, they will not harm you in any way. It is stated that many of the Yogis of India can walk uninjured through dense jungles filled with tigers and venomous snakes". This also throws a new and interesting light on the Old Testament account of Daniel in the lions' den.

Carrington also said - 'Between animals and ourselves there is doubtless a link which unites us all into one conscious whole; this being the life of the universe which runs through every sentient thing'.

Could it be that it is because the Churches seem to be losing sight of this all important central fact that they are also losing much of their power?

Edgar Cayce speaking in trance on the subject of religion would seem to confirm this when he said 'There is no way to glorify God in worship or devotion which sets Him apart from His creation. His presence is to be found 'in', 'with', 'under' all of His creation; and efforts to limit God's presence to sacred things, times, places would merely quench the spirit'.

Perhaps the one thing most responsible, or should I say perhaps most used by Christians to excuse Man's treatment of the animal kingdom is the comment in the story of the creation that God gave man dominion over the animals. What is forgotten is that dominion means charge of, caring for, a responsibility for their welfare. It does not bestow 'carte blanche' to do as we please with them.

Those who would use the Bible to uphold their treatment of animals should look a little deeper, for throughout the books of both testaments we come across admonitions to treat our animal friends with kindness and justice, such as Proverbs 12.10. 'The Just regardeth the lives of his beasts, but the heart of the wicked is cruel'.

Throughout the Bible there are innumerable little homilies on day to day kind treatment. For example, Deuteronomy 22.10. 'Thou shalt not plough with an ox and an ass together'. Why not? Because the yoke would not be evenly distributed. And again, in Deuteronomy, 'Thou shalt not muzzle the ox that treadeth out the corn'. Corn was thrashed by driving oxen through it, naturally they would snatch the old mouthful as they went and the above text makes it clear that they should be allowed this small 'perk' as they work. In the comprehensive instructions for the keeping of the Sabbath in Exodus we find the words 'That thy ox and thy ass may rest'.

The above passages make it clear that we are expected not only to feed and house our animals but to give them the opportunity to enjoy the pleasures that are available to them in life.

If, throughout the Bible, there are injunctions to care for animals then how can practising Christians sanction such cruel exploitation of animals for sport and gain as bull-fighting, vivisection and many of the practices of modern factory-farming?

It is all too easy to blame 'The Church' as a corporate body for not speaking out against the atrocities that man commits against the animal world. I have done so myself, feeling that the 'little' people, Mr & Mrs Everyman, were already kind the animals and would be even kinder if only the Church would tell them to be so.

My researches revealed a different story, however. It is not the Church leaders in the main who are silent, it is rather that their words fall on deaf ears.

Pope St Pius V called bullfighting 'the most degrading of pastimes, a spectacle for demons rather than men' and he excommunicated all who took part in it. Strong enough words one would imagine from a revered head of the largest Christian Church in the world. Yet many years later - in what are commonly believed to be more enlightened times – we find a Jesuit priest writing, 'The Church has not condemned bull-fighting as immoral' and going on to defend it by saying that it is more "natural" than boxing and that it is not blood-lust that excites the crowd!

In the 19th. Century there was no louder or clearer voice speaking against vivisection than His Eminence Cardinal Manning. As vice-president of the British society against vivisection he was a tireless and outspoken speaker and was absolutely unequivocal in his condemnation of the practice.

"Between sanctioning its atrocities and stopping the practice altogether there is no middle course". He said in one of his speeches, adding - "By prohibiting vivisection you will at one and the same time save numberless animals from pangs which add no small item to the sum of misery upon earth, and men from acquiring that hardness of heart and deadness of conscience for which the most brilliant discovery of physiology would be poor compensation".

Today, a hundred or so years after his death, vivisection is still carried on - on a scale the immensity of which was undreamed of in his day.

On Easter Day 1980 Pope John Paul II announced that St Francis had been officially proclaimed patron saint of the ecological movement in a papal bull. An announcement which received extraordinarily little comment or publicity from the press, the Church or anyone else for that matter.

On November 11th 1981 the Pope received a large audience of pilgrims among whom where members of The League of St Francis led by the man who founded it some 20 years ago in Venice, Monsignor Fusaro. The league seeks to defend nature and animals, particularly through education. After his general greeting to the many pilgrims in several languages the Pope greeted the League in the following words "I greet especially the members of The League of St Francis - I am very pleased to be with you esteemed ecologists and I am glad to give encouragement in the work that you undertake to safeguard the heritage of nature and the protection of animals, our little brothers. May the Lord bless you and abundantly reward you for your noble and praiseworthy work".

It seems his words have permeated so little into the vast body of the Church that a parish priest, a member of The Franciscan order, can only find to say about St Francis that 'he was kind to animals' and admit that he had never thought of preaching that same kindness from the pulpit of his church or teaching it to school children to whom he regularly gave Religious Instruction!

Kindness to animals however, while good, is not going to be enough to save our world. Pope John Paul, saw this when he decreed that St Franics should be the patron saint of ecologists.

In its widest sense ecology means accepting dominion over the earth by caring for it, and its creatures. St Francis knew this eight centuries ago. As materialism and science sweep us relentlessly forward it is imperative that we stop, listen, and learn.

Christianity places much stress on the Life Hereafter - suffering on this earth will be rewarded with bliss in the next world. At the same time many theologians have actually put forward the view that because animals have no souls, and therefore no hope of another life, it is quite pardonable and not at all sinful to treat them as we will in this world.

What a superb example of muddled thinking, blind hypocrisy and sheer arrogance! Surely quite the reverse is true. If this earthly life is indeed all that the animal world can look forward to, then it is up to us to see it is an enjoyable one - not a hell of suffering and exploitation.

The existence - or otherwise - of the soul of an animal is surely irrelevant when considering cruelty. For we know quite well they are sentient creatures who feel pain and suffer just as we do.

If we really study the lives and teachings of many of the great saints of the Church we will see that they did not merely advocate a kindness that is merely the absence of cruelty or at best giving a dog an absent-minded pat on the head. They taught a positive caring, a sharing with them in the love and worship of God and a sort of daily partnership.

Lecky, the historian, in his book *History of European Morals*, pin-pointed this attitude very well. When writing about monastic farming he said 'It represents one of the most striking efforts made in Christendom to inculcate a feeling of kindness and pity toward the brute creation' and 'The religious man becomes gentle, moderate and humane in the tribute of work he expects from his animals. He sees in them the companions of his labours, and he takes good care not to cut them off from his affection and compassion'.

A 13th century rule laid down by the Abbey of St Peter, Gloucester, expressly states that the servants of their manors are to take care of the oxen, making sure that the mangers in each stall contain a night's food for each team, and they are to plough without injuring or distressing the beasts.

Having looked briefly at the Church's teaching on animals in the past but what of the present?

In many of the people I talked to I found a curious sort of detachment for want of a better word, as if the animal world were as detached from our own as another planet. Perhaps our modern civilisation has something to do with this?

People simply do not realise how closely their own lives are interwoven with that of the animals who share this earth with us. For so many people their closest contact with animals is with the meat on their plates. How many children (or adults for that matter) connect the sterilised carton of milk in the supermarket with the cow in the paddock?

Too many people are too busy to bother about animals and too blind, alas, to see any connection between the two.

In 1929 a group of Catholics and Christians of various other denominations met regularly in London to organise united prayer for the Humane movement. Realising the enormous contribution their Church could make to the cause of kindness to animals if it promulgated the teachings of the saints, the Bible and the Church itself, tentative moves were made by the Catholics in the group to start a society for this purpose.

It was, however, 1935 before the first public meeting was held. The first thing the new group did was issue a bulletin, and so their magazine "*The Ark*" was born.

The new group was given ecclesiastical approval from the beginning and successive Archbishops of Westminster have consented to accept the Presidency.

The main purpose of the group, who called themselves The Catholic Study Circle for Animal Welfare, is to help the Humane Movement by personal and organised prayer, by research into the writings of people in authority, such as Popes, Cardinals etc, and the publication of their findings and by offering their journal '*The Ark*' as a forum for airing views on the whole humane question.

Today the society is internationally known with branches in many of the world's leading countries, America, Canada, France, Ireland and Australia to name a few and it campaigns ceaselessly for a fair deal for the animal world and the abolition of cruelty and injustice towards the creatures which are under our dominion. It works in close co-operation wherever possible with animal societies that are engaged in more practical matters. Christians of every denomination are among its members, so it is truly ecumenical.

In England, the Quakers, a people always associated with their concern for peace and the rights of the oppressed, also have a group concerned with the welfare of animals.

As we move forward into the Aquarian Age when, if we are to believe the seers and prophets, organised religion will undergo a gradual change; moving away from the concept of 'The Church' as a physical entity where land and buildings, schools, hospitals and colleges play an important part, into what must surely be nearer to the Church envisioned by its founder - a spiritual entity where men are bound together by spiritual ideals rather than by allegiance to a creed. Perhaps as we move into such a time we shall see the animal world more openly cared for and protected by Christianity. Let us hope that this happens before too long.

Although this chapter is on animals and Christianity - not Animals and Religion, for that subject alone would cover a book at least – it is necessary to touch, however briefly, on the place of animals in other faiths. For just as 'no man is an island' so is no religion, least of all Christianity with its passion for missionising.

It is a tragic reflection on the Christian Church that, as its missionaries fan across Asia converting Hindus and Buddhists, whose religion teaches them a reverence for all life, we teach them not only to eat meat and thus kill for food but to sell for gain their innocent wildlife, such as the millions of Asian monkeys used in the vivisection laboratories of the world. Surely such sacrifice must be seen by the Creator as so many crucifixions - only this time it is not even the souls of men to be saved - but their bodies.

I think perhaps one of the most poignant and telling condemnations I have heard of Christianity - a faith which knows about caring for our animal friends but fails to teach it - was made almost unknowingly by the commentator on a TV. documentary on a Tibetan community. Remarking on the tameness and lack of fear of the wild birds he made the observation "The birds here are quite tame and unafraid of people - for this is a Buddhist community".

It is of interest to note what the Jewish faith has to say, about animals. Christianity is, to a certain extent, based on the Jewish faith. Jesus was himself a Jew and the books of the Old Testament which contain the history and the beliefs of the Jewish people form part of the Christian Bible. As we have already seen there are many, many injunctions in the Old

Testament to treat animals that are in our care with kindness and consideration.

The Bible tells us that God made the beasts of the earth according to their kinds, and cattle, and everything that creepeth on the earth according to its kind. And God saw it was good.

Having created them we are told constantly of God's caring for them, the story of Noah's Ark is just one example, and as Jesus himself pointed out when speaking of the birds - "They do not sow or reap or gather into barns, yet your father feeds them".

What could be plainer than the simple injunction - "Hast thou cattle? Have a care for them". (Ecclus. 7.24). And again in Exodus, 23, 4 & 5. 'Thou shalt not pass by if thou see thy brother's ox or ass go astray, but thou shalt bring it back to thy brother. If thou shalt see thy enemy's ox or ass going astray, bring it back to him. If thou shalt see the ass of him that hateth thee lie underneath his burden thou shalt not pass by, but shalt lift him up'.

That wonderful phrase - 'Thou shalt not pass by' should by the slogan of all who profess Christianity in their dealings with animal suffering.

We are told that the rewards of caring for animals will be abundant life for ourselves.

"If thou find as thou walkest by the way a bird's nest on the ground and the dam sitting on the young, let her go - that it may be well with thee and thou mayest living a long time'. (Deut. 22.6.)

With such a clear injunction how can we expect to prolong life for mankind by the mutilation and torture of our fellow creatures in research laboratories?

Speaking on this topic, a modern Jew, Rabbi Sidney J. Jacobs, who was one of the speakers at a rally for 'The Liberation of Animals in Laboratories' in Los Angeles in October 1980, said:

"My own religion is forceful in its prohibition of cruelty against animals. The Hebrew Scriptures, Talmud and Response literature, are all specific in condemning the 'suffering of living things'. Jewish tradition carries this concern for animals in its unqualified negative stance against hunting".

Spiritualists believe that animals possess a spirit and at least two books have been written on the subject of animals in the afterlife by practising Spiritualists, "Animals In The Spirit World" by Harold Sharp and "When an Animal Dies" by Sylvia Barbanell.

Putting the belief in the spirituality of animals as well as their 'animalness' into practice in daily life, many spiritualists are also vegetarians and many who are healers will use their gifts as much for the welfare of animals as for people.

Many mediums allow their cats or dogs to be present during a seance for they believe that they have a strong magnetic influence and give power - thus adding to the success of the seance.

Perhaps the 'Blessing of the Animals' services that are held in some Churches, both Catholic and Anglican in many parts of the world to commemorate St Francis, reflect a growing awareness of the truth expressed in the Edgar Cayce trance readings: "There is no way to glorify God in worship or devotion which sets Him apart from His creation". Perhaps these special services, ostensibly to bless the animals, will, in fact, invoke a special blessing on mankind.

Chapter Four

Animal Magic

The dividing line between religion and magic has been very thin down the ages, where it has existed at all. In Egypt the two were inextricably woven, as they were in Roman times.

With less of today's technology to separate people from close contact with Nature and the animal world we find animals played a much greater part in religious rites. Some of these seem to have been extraordinarily wasteful to say the least of it, certainly when looked at in the light of present-day farming practices.

One Roman religious rite, known as The Sacred Spring, involved the sacrifice to Jupiter of all cattle, sheep, pigs and goats born in the months of March and April. As these months are the Spring - peak of reproductive activity - in the Northern hemisphere this would mean a good proportion of the farm stock!

In March – the month named for Mars, the god of war - the Romans held important horse races in the Campus Martius. These had a two-fold purpose, for in addition to entertainment and the training of the cavalry horses it was also believed that so much energy expended would benefit the spring crops.

In the autumn an important event took place called 'The October Horse'. This was a chariot race, also held in honour of the God Mars. One horse from the winning team was stabbed to death in honour of the God. Its head and tail were then cut off, the head garlanded with bread and fought for by two teams made up of men from rival areas of the city. The winners then hoisted the head up in triumph in their own area. This strange rite was, in actual fact, a fertility rite and was believed to ensure good crops the following year.

Meanwhile the tail of the horse was taken by a runner to Regia, former palace of the kings of Rome. There it was hung so that the blood from it dripped on the hearth where it was collected by the Vestal Virgins and kept till the following April when it was used in the ritual purification of the cattle.

Out in the Roman countryside farmers, together with their families and labourers, would ceremoniously walk the boundaries of their land once a year. They wore olive wreaths and clean white clothes and their oxen were garlanded. A male lamb was led around in front of them three times before being ritually sacrificed to Bacchus, the God of the grapes, and Ceres, the corn Goddess, who were requested to protect both the land and the cattle to ensure the fertility of both.

In fact, most of these old religious rites were fertility rites. There was also the one enacted each February when young men went to a cave on the Palatine Hill called the Lupercal, or place of the wolf. It was believed that it was here that the She-wolf had suckled Romulus and Remus, the legendary founders of the city of Rome.

The young men sacrificed a dog and some goats and smeared themselves with the blood which they wiped off with wool or goat's hair dipped in milk. Then, naked except for girdles made of skins of the sacrificed animals and holding strips of goat's hide, they ran around the boundaries of the old city (I should imagine they needed to keep warm!) slapping those they met with the pieces of hide. The purpose of all this was to induce fertility in barren women and ensure an easy childbirth. The young men themselves were often referred to as he-goats.

Most Roman festivities seem to have been accompanied by the sacrifice of domestic animals and seem to us gory, but no doubt to a people used for their entertainment to the Colosseum and the throwing of Christians to lions and similar entertainment no doubt they were not seen as 'bloody' at all but quite within the norm.

Were they, one wonders, also symbolic of Pan - half goat, half man - so often invoked in medieval fertility rites?

The Romans also had what was known as a College of Augurs. The job of an augur was to determine the portents of signs and omens and what was of national importance. The augur was a priest of the gods, he wore a white robe and carried a staff called a Litus. This was a long wand with a curved piece bending over at the top, very like a Bishop's crook. In fact, some people hold that the bishop's crook is a direct descendant of the Litus of the Roman Augur.

The priest would pray to the Gods then peer through the curved bit of his Litus. Whatever animal or bird he saw through this would be interpreted as the answer of the Gods. If he saw it to the right it meant good fortune, to the left, bad. In fact, it is from this ritual that we get our word sinister which is taken from the Latin 'on the left', meaning boding ill.

Many old superstitions regarding animals and birds that are with us to this day probably come down from Roman times, such as this verse about magpies:

> One for sorrow, two for joy
> Three for wedding, four for a birth
> Five for silver, six for gold
> And seven for a secret never told.

In their little book 'The Wiccan Guide to Witches Ways' published in 1980, Clair and Simon Lorde, two present-day witches claim this magpie verse as a Wiccan verse. They devote a page and a half to auguries, for instance, if you hear an owl hooting beware. If it's before midnight it means that trouble is on the way, after midnight and before dawn it can signify death.

Owls have always had a close association with the occult and the mysterious, probably because of their air of and reputation for wisdom and 'all-knowing', aided and abetted by their amazing eyes which help to make them appear 'all-seeing'. Add to this the fact that, like cats, they are also creatures of the night, and we can understand the awe that their air of mystery instils.

There are many superstitions and legends about owls; to see an owl silhouetted against a full moon is a certain warning of death and/or disaster.

There is also a belief held by Canadian Indians that the owl calls the name of a person before they die. A beautiful little book has been written around this belief called "I heard the owl call my name". It's about a young clergymen with a terminal illness who spends the end of his days among these Indians and it tells how much he learns from them about the true meaning of life and death.

On the subject of naming a cat, the poet, T.S. Elliot in his light-hearted book of poems about cats devoted a whole poem to this problem. In it he declared that every cat must have at least three names – one sensible, one peculiar and one known only to itself and the gods.

"But above and beyond there's still one left over,
And that is the name that you never will guess;
The name that no human research can discover
BUT THE CAT HIMSELF KNOWS, and will never confess.

This is a reminder of the old legend that every living soul has its own secret name and to learn it gives one complete power over that person. There can be few, I think, who have stumbled on the secret name of a cat – for of all creatures she is surely the most 'her own person'!

Apart from her historical links with the deities of Ancient Egypt the cat has always seemed feminine and mysterious. She is the only domestic animal we have never really succeeded in taming, she is always 'her own person'. It's no wonder we still connect her with the occult.

When I was a small child living in rural England there was a little old lady who kept a small shop (the only one) in our tiny hamlet. I use the word 'little' in its physical sense – she was tiny. I am sure there was nothing little about her in other ways.

Her shop, which was totally unlike any other shop, fascinated me. It consisted of the back room, the scullery really, of her cottage. To get to it you crossed a little green off the road, up a narrow path with overhanging greenery and round the corner, through her back garden to the back door. Half-way up the path I always got a deliciously exciting sensation of mystery and danger which stayed with me till I was safely back on the country land at the front of the cottage.

Whatever the weather, even in the hottest and brightest summer day, the back garden was dark, cool and shivery. This was due, no doubt, to the tall hedge which had been allowed to grow as high as the cottage itself and to the huge gnarled old yew tree which grew in the middle of the small patch of dank grass that passed as a lawn and cast its sombre shadow over everything.

Once in the back yard it was usually necessary to knock on the door to summon Mrs. Walters to her scullery shop. Here she sold sweets, chocolate, biscuits, bread etc, using an old hanging spring balance scales with a dial and a large brass pan to measure out her goodies. Even though this contraption hung just over the scrubbed kitchen table she used as a counter she was so small that she had to stand on a box to see the dial, and to read this she used a large Sherlock Holmes type of magnifying glass.

The purchase of a penny worth of sweets involved a ritual that never lost its fascination for me.

Mrs. Walters was popularly held by the country people to be a witch. She certainly looked like one, and to lend further credence to the belief, she always had a large family of very well-fed cats. Stray cats in the district always knew where to go. My father said that the cats put up some sort of a secret sign to inform any wandering feline in search of a home that this was the place to stay, in much the same way that gipsies are said to leave a secret sign to others at a gateway where people who will provide a meal or shelter. I implicitly believed him.

One of her cats was an enormous black and white long-haired tom. Every so often he would come stalking into our farmyard, about half a mile from his home – probably in search of females – and pick a quarrel with our diminutive Yorkshire terrier cross dog, Mickey. Mickey's valour was much larger than his person. He was, in fact, only about two-thirds the size of the cat, and invariably came off worse in these scraps. We would hastily hustle him indoors when Tom, in martial mood, was seen approaching.

Tom must, I think, have been her familiar. He was certainly undisputed boss animal, dog or cat, of our tiny hamlet. His predecessor had been a dog.

He was like the one that rode on my shoulder when I was cross. His name was Carlo and he was black, at least so I was told. I never knew Carlo though, like everyone in the neighbourhood, I was familiar with his grave.

He was buried under the Yew tree and if Mrs. Walters took a liking to you, she honoured you by pointing it out. A favourite uncle was staying with us once, and came with me on an errand for my mother to buy biscuits. Intrigued by the little old lady and her unique shop, he set about charming her and 'drawing her out'. She was charmed - and rewarded him by not only showing him Carlo's grave, but regaling him with details of his burial.

"I made a brand new shroud for him" she told us, "and buried him just here, beneath the Yew tree". Her voice dropped, "At night - by moonlight - and," she added in a sibilant whisper, "I am sure I put a brand-new florin (a two shilling piece) in the grave with him!"

Somehow the story made such an impression on me that forever after I found myself casting surreptitious glances over my shoulder to the stone beneath the Yew tree that marked the dog's grave.

Whether my uncle asked the meaning of the florin, I do not know. If he did I did not hear the answer - so absorbed was I in the spine-chilling account of the midnight burial.

It was many, many years later that I came across the ancient belief that unless a coin of some sort was placed with a body in the grave, the spirit would be unable to cross the waters of The Styx to reach the other shore - and eternal life – for the ferryman would not take anyone across in his boat who did not have money for the fare.

It is universally accepted that pure black cats are lucky and the reverse is often held of white cats, so much so that some people will refuse to give house room to a pure white cat. A cat with extra toes is considered especially lucky and in the north of England the tortoiseshell cat is considered to be the best possible insurance against fire.

When it comes to colour in animals, horses too come in for their share of superstition.

Knights of old, including St George, always rode a pure white charger. Yet curiously enough, it was held to be unlucky to meet a white horse, but not if you didn't see its tail. In other words, if it was going in the opposite direction. I wonder if it is a relic of this old superstition that, in horsy circles, there simply is no such thing as a white horse. However snowy its coat such a horse is always correctly termed 'grey'.

To see a piebald horse on the road meant good fortune, provided you remembered to wish before its tail went out of sight. Black horses, that is pure black, were shunned and deemed by many people to be as dark within as they were without. Perhaps their connection with funerals and death was the cause for this.

Horses with wall eyes, that is one brown and one blue, were often deemed lucky – particularly in Wales – which no doubt accounts for the prevalence of wall eyes in some strains of Welsh ponies.

White socks, that is white markings on the foot and lower leg, were considered lucky if there weren't too many; "One buy him, two try him, three suspect him, four reject him" goes the old jingle. Also, they were socks – white stockings extended above the knee were said to be unlucky and to denote weakness in that leg.

Animals, of course, have always been associated with luck, both good and bad.

Perhaps it is no accident that one of the makes of car which symbolises wealth and success in today's world for so many people is the Jaguar with the figure of this animal as its symbol. It is in the form of a Jaguar that the all-powerful sun god has appeared down the ages, and still does, in many diverse cultures.

We are all familiar with the three wise monkeys: Hear-no-evil, Speak-no-evil and See-no-evil, but among the ruins of an Egyptian temple dedicated to Ra-Hor-Ackty (The Rising Sun) was found the statue of four monkeys. In ancient Egypt the tradition was long held that monkeys always greet the dawn.

The Chiriguani Indians of South America have a legend about a fabulous green tiger-god that eats the sun and the moon during an eclipse. The same tiger perhaps that Forest Indians in Peru believe existed as a star in the sky?

Among the many mysteries of the world are the vast 'drawings' of animals, insects and birds which ancient people's made on the earth's surface. The white horses of England are probably the most widely known.

Even more strange, though, are the vast figures of birds, animals and insects 'drawn' on the dried-up desert of Peru, presumably by the Nasacans a pre-Inca civilisation. These drawings, so large that they can only be seen from the air, are a complete enigma. The spider, for instance, is 150 feet long. Why should a civilisation that existed so long before Man's conquest of flight go to so much trouble to draw pictures that can only be appreciated from the air?

Mixed in among the drawings are several extraordinarily accurate geometrical straight lines. These do not appear to have any astronomical value and, apart from the fact that they often seem to begin or end at the reproductive part of the animal – which suggests some connection with a fertility rite – they appear to lead nowhere.

The Nascans were obviously deeply involved with animals and nature, for all their pottery shows this life force motif. Birds, fish, insects, animals or flowers and sprouting seeds. Many have an almost humourous, certainly happy, connotation and some are extraordinarily 'modern' in appearance – such as a design that depicts a duck with corn cobs drawn over, or in, his body giving a very well-stuffed appearance!

While many of our old beliefs and superstitions are shrouded in mystery, one thing is certain, throughout history, animals have played an important part in 'Man's Magic'.

Chapter Five

In Myth & Legend

There can be few animals, with the exception of the cat, whose air of mystery has caused him to appear in so many stories of myth and magic, who figures so much in superstition and legend, as the donkey.

Most well-known is probably the story of how the donkey got the cross on his back. The story goes that ever since a donkey carried Jesus into Jerusalem on Palm Sunday, a journey that was to end in the crucifixion, he has born the cross over his own shoulders. A charming legend but, in actual fact, the dorsal stripe or 'cross' is also worn by wild horses and by some domestic breeds of dun or buckskin horses. And, of course, a great many mules also have this distinctive mark.

Almost all the legends and superstitions about donkeys are connected with Christianity, such as the widely held belief that at midnight on Christmas Eve donkeys and cattle drop to their knees for a brief second of homage and remembrance of that first Christmas when they shared the stable with the new-born Christ Child.

Another supersession from this first Christmas is that the ovals of soft skin on the inside of every donkey's front legs – just above the knee – which are quite different to the horny 'chestnuts' on a horse's legs, are the marks left by Mary when she reached out and gripped the donkey's leg to pull herself up from the straw of the stable floor after the birth of Jesus.

Country people in Ireland often call these marks "Our Lady's thumbprints".

Pictures of St Anthony often show him with a kneeling donkey. This is illustrating the story of how the saint once said that he would not believe in the presence of Christ in the Holy Eucharist unless his ass knelt down before it. And, of course, that is just what the pious donkey did! Balaam's ass in the Bible who saw the angel of God when his master did not is, of course, well-known.

It was the custom in the Middle Ages in French churches to commemorate the Flight into Egypt by leading a donkey, covered in rich trappings and ridden by a young girl carrying either a doll or a live baby through the streets, into the Church and up the aisle where it remained throughout the Mass.

With so many superstitions and legends connecting it with the Christian Faith one would expect the donkey to be respected and even revered instead of which we find it much more often the butt of ridicule than honour.

The writers of fables, Aesop and much later the French poet La Fontaine who lived in the 17th. century, wrote fables featuring donkeys. Aesop's most famous donkey was probably the one who was always dissatisfied. When it was summer he wished it were winter and vice versa; whatever the conditions prevailing at the time he wished for something different and therefore never enjoyed anything.

La Fontaine wrote an entertaining story about a lion, a monkey and two donkeys. The monkey recounts to the lion a conversation he overheard between two donkeys in which, he says, they were "Offering the incense of flattery to each other by turns".

"Do you not think that Man, that 'perfect' animal is both unjust and stupid?" says the first ass. "He profanes our august name by calling everyone of his own kind an ass who is ignorant or dull or idiotic; and he calls our laughter and our discourse by the term 'braying'. It is very amusing that these human people pretend to excel us!"

The point of the story is, of course, that we all tend to think that those unlike ourselves are inferior.

La Fontaine also tells a story about two mules who are travelling together with laden packs. One is carrying a load of silver coins and the other oats. The one carrying the silver is boasting that he is entrusted with such a valuable load when they are attacked by robbers. The silver is stolen but the oats are left untouched. The moral of that little tale being that it doesn't always do to boast about our valuable possessions.

We have all heard and, no doubt, used the saying 'As stubborn as a mule' and probably many of the other sayings and proverbs in common use about donkeys. 'He/she can talk the hind legs off a donkey'; 'I wouldn't go within an ass's roar of them (it).' 'One ass nicknames another Longears'.

Almost without exception these proverbs show the humble donkey in a derogatory light. 'If an ass goes travelling he'll not come home a horse.' 'The braying of an ass does not reach Heaven' and so on. All in much the same vein. I only know of one of these common sayings that gives the donkey any credit at all: 'Better the ass that carries you than the horse that throws you!'

One of the most popular beliefs or superstitions among country people is that 'You will never see a dead donkey.' Unhappily not true, for donkeys, like everyone else, are mortal. Another superstition is that it is very unlucky to kill a donkey. Both these have their foundation, no doubt, in the fact that the skull of a donkey is not anatomically identical to that of the horse, making it more difficult to find the correct spot when putting down a donkey so that the bullet from the humane killer will go directly into the brain and not simply shatter bone. To support the first of these beliefs donkeys do live longer than horses; 40 being quite common and even greater ages than this have been recorded, while a horse lives to around 30.

Another belief held in parts of rural Ireland is that donkeys will, if they feel life has become worthless, commit suicide and tales are told in the West of Ireland of donkeys simply walking out to sea to their death.

A donkey in fiction who may well be said to be taking her place in legend is Violetta from Paul Gallico's enchanting story "*Never Take No For An Answer*', also filmed as '*The Small Miracle*'. It's about the little boy whose only friend in the world, and also his only means of earning a living, was his donkey Violetta. When she became sick it was a major disaster for him and he sought permission to take her to the crypt of St Francis of Assissi. (The story is set in Italy.) His request is refused and he works steadily up the hierarchy of the Church until he gets to the Pope himself who finally gives permission and Violetta is cured.

In direct contrast to the donkey, the horse in myth or legend is usually shown as super horse, or not entirely horse. Best known of these are the Centaur, half man and half horse; Pegasus, the winged horse; and of course, the mythical Unicorn, the horse with one horn.

The white horse in legend has become symbolic of romance, chivalry and purity. Strange, for in real life all white horses are actually old grey horses! In the best fairytales Prince Charming always rides to the rescue of the damsel in distress on a pure white charger. The knight of cups, representing romantic love in the tarot cards is, in most decks, depicted as a handsome young prince astride a pure white horse.

We see the same symbolism appearing in the twentieth century in Western films. The 'goody' always rides a white (or at least very light coloured) horse while the 'baddies' ride dark horses. Most famous of these modern-day chivalrous knights is Hopalong Cassidy, beloved of at least 2 generations of children in the first half of the 20th. century who always rode to the rescue on a white horse.

Just as the unfortunate donkey always tends to be depicted as the silly ass, which anyone who knows anything about donkeys will know is quite unjust, and the horse as a sort of super being, so the cat is usually depicted as sagacious, wise, even cunning, qualities. These he often uses on behalf of his human friends or friend – not master, for it is not in the nature of the cat to call any man master!

Typical examples of this are Dick Whittington's cat and Puss in Boots, both of whom by the adroit use of their considerable wits helped their human friends to attain fame and fortune. In so doing, of course, they considerably improved their own material position in life.

Most stories of dogs and cats in legend tend to uphold the saying that "Dogs drool and cats rule". The relationship between man and dog goes back at least 10,000 years, possibly more. There is a charming legend that tells how this enduring relationship began.

When God first created the world and all living creatures, a great chasm opened up separating Man from all the other creatures. When the dog saw this he realised that he was about to be separated from Man forever and he leapt across the gap just before it widened too much and took his place beside Man, where he has remained ever since.

The Lapps, to whom the service of the dog is invaluable in controlling their herds of reindeer, say that in the beginning the dog was aligned with the wolf against Man but he decided to throw in his lot with Man but in doing so lost the power of speech. However he retained the ability to read Man's thoughts and to understand everything that was said to him.

Indeed, The Lapps who believe that everything was created by the same God, have some interesting traditions about animals. One is that on a man's death the animals he has known in life will be called in first to pass judgement on him and only when they have had their say will humans be asked their opinion.

They also believe that a bear will not hurt a woman. Axel Munthe relates how, when he was travelling with a young woman as guide, they met a bear in the forest. She promptly pulled up her tunic to show the wide breeches that Lapp women wore as part of their costume and the bear turned and walked away.

In many countries where elephants are common it is believed that they have their own religion, worshipping superior beings represented by the sun and the moon. Many people have reported seeing elephants (and other animals) standing silently as if in prayer at dawn and sunset facing the rising or setting sun. One traveller in West Africa wrote: "I was shown monkeys, known as guerezas, sitting just so every dawn and dusk, on the tops of the highest jungle trees, and all invariably facing the coming or going of the sun. Witnessing this gave me an uneasy feeling of awe so that I went, day after day, to watch, and soon found myself 'praying' with them."

Then there's the story about St Francis and the wolf of Gubbio. The saint, so the story goes, was living in the city of Gubbio at the time when an enormous and ferocious wolf appeared in the area killing and devouring not only goats and sheep but cattle and even human beings. Things got so bad that no-one dared leave the city and St Francis, feeling sorry for the good people of Gubbio, volunteered to go out to where the wolf had his lair and see what he could do. He was followed at a very discreet distance by many of the townspeople, anxious to witness what they devoutly hoped would be a miracle of some sort.

The wolf came at St Francis with an open mouth but, instead of turning and fleeing, the good man made the sign of the cross and actually called him saying; "Come along Brother Wolf, I command you on the part of Christ, that you do no harm to me or anyone!"

Promptly the wolf closed his terrible mouth, stopped running and came quietly, gentle as a lamb, and lay down at St Francis' feet.

St Francis then talked to him quietly, admonished him for the terrible things he had done, telling him that he deserved to be hung on a gallows like a convict but promised him that if he would make peace with the townspeople he, St Francis, would see that he was pardoned and neither men nor dogs would harangue him in the future. All the time he was talking to him the saint called him Brother Wolf.

When the wolf accepted this, St Francis went even further and told him that if he kept his promise not to molest animals or people he would see that the men of the city provided food for him as long as he lived.

The wolf agreed once more and St Francis said; "Brother Wolf I would have you pledge me your faith that you will keep this promise". He held out his hand to the wolf who immediately placed his paw in his palm. The two then walked together into the city and St Francis spoke to the people saying that the wolf had promised not to hurt anyone again and that, in turn, he had promised that he would not be molested by the people of the town but would be fed by them. St Francis added that he would go surety for the wolf. Then, turning to the animal, he asked him to repeat his pledge before the citizens of Gubbio and once more the wolf put his right paw into St Francis right hand.

For two more years the wolf lived in the city neither molesting nor being molested and even so, we are told, going peaceably on social visits into the homes of the citizens. When he died of old age the citizens grieved for him for while he lived amongst them he was a constant reminder of the goodness of St Francis.

The Tarot cards are packed with archetypal images and figures from myth and legend, all of which speak directly to our subconscious. Not the least symbolic of these images are the animals that figure in our present day Tarot decks.

Best known and most popular of today's Tarot cards is the Rider Waite pack and in these cards alone we find no less than five white horses: the Knight of Swords as well as the Knight of Cups is mounted on a white horse; the rider bearing the laurel wreath of victory in the 6 of rods is on a white horse; as is the armoured skeleton in the Death card. In the card of the Sun, a young child is seen astride a white horse. Although these cards may seem very different on the surface the symbolic white horse has much the same message in all of them – he stands for purity, energy, and hope.

The other two knights in the deck are also mounted but the Knight of Rods is astride an orange coloured horse as befits the Fire knight while the earthy knight of Pentacles rides a strong earthy looking black steed.

We have the lion on the Strength card, but a relatively gentle and subdued lion symbolising strength more of an inner, spiritual sort than a rampant physical force. Heraldic lions also appear on the throne of the King of Rods who, of course, represents the astrological sign of Leo. There's a lion's head in the bottom right hand corner of the World card and a winged lion in the same position on the Wheel of Fortune. Here the lion is representing the element Fire.

On the Queen of Rods card we find lions carved into the arms of her throne and a domestic black cat sitting in front of her. We can see the cat as having the powerful forces of the lion transmuted into domesticity under the influence of the Queen and also as representing the moon and thus the mystical and feminine side of the Queen of Rods.

We find three cards that feature the dog. Best known of course is that of The Fool who has a small white dog at his heel jumping up, apparently to warn him as he is about to step blithely into the chasm at his feet. Here the dog represents our conscience, our inner self, whatever it is that alerts us to mistakes we might make in our journey through life.

In the 10 of Pentacles we see two gentle looking domestic dogs symbolising home and family enjoying the worldly wealth of the humans in the card. In the Moon we have both a dog and a wolf baying at the moon. These two canines symbolise the two sides of Man's nature and the inevitable struggle between them, while behind them a scorpion is rising from the water suggesting that a wrong choice can mean being pulled back into the mire.

Other water creatures are shown with the Page and the King of Cups. The fish, we remember, was the symbol of the early Christians and a fish in the Page's cup represents spiritual awakening. Behind the King of Cups is a dolphin showing that though he appears to be worldly and all powerful the

King of Cups, who represents Scorpio, also has a psychic/spiritual side.

The hooded falcon on the hand of the richly dressed person on the 9 of Pentacles card has much the same message. Birds, in general, represent spirituality and the presence of it in this card says that however well one may do in life it is as well to remember the spiritual side and the fact that the falcon is hooded and under the control of the woman on the card shows that we should not only be aware of this side of our nature but to a certain extent be in control of it.

Thus, merely by flicking through a deck of Tarot cards we can see how animals have been used in their mythical and legendary roles to convey important truths about both the world outside and our own inner selves and that their role is deeper and of greater significance than as mere fairy-tale characters.

Chapter Six

Animal Ghosts

There can be few people who live with dogs who have not had the unnerving experience at some time or another of their dog 'seeing' something, or someone, invisible to them.

Many years ago, I was working in a small hotel on the island of Guernsey, one of the Channel Islands between England and France. It was a beautiful old stone house mellowed by time and exuding an aura of peace and serenity. However, at the back of the house in the extensive garden was another building, an old stone barn. This was used as a store room for things like potatoes. The owners of the hotel had a Siamese cat and a beautiful German Shepherd called Rudolph. The cat was never seen in the shed (much to their chagrin as mice were!) and Rudolph flatly refused to enter it.

He would usually trot down the garden path with me, for we were good friends and I often took him for walks round the island lanes, but when we got to the doorway of the shed he would stand there, staring at a point somewhere in the back of the shed with his ruff on end and his lip curled back in a snarl. As he was the most lovable and cheerful dog this was most uncharacteristic behaviour.

When I remarked on his behaviour I was told "He can probably see the ghost. There is an old story that someone was murdered in that shed about two hundred years ago"!

If dogs can SEE ghosts then it seems quite logical to assume that they can also BE ghosts. In the literature of the supernatural they certainly seem to be almost as numerous as they are on the earthly plane.

Dog ghosts appear to be roughly divided between the comforting and the terrifying and, particularly in the latter, a thread of similarity seems to link them from age to age and country to country.

Legends of ghostly black dogs abound especially in all parts of the British Isles. Conan Doyle is said to have based his famous story "The Hound of The Baskervilles" on an old Dorset legend of a phantom dog which in turn is based on the Danish Hound of Odin. Going further back we find Anubis of the Ancient Egyptians, guard god-dog of the dead.

So widespread are the legends and stories of black dogs that it's possible they are part of our collective unconscious, the dark pool of beliefs and knowledge that Jung believed were common to whole races and tribes of people. Perhaps this is what my father was tapping into when he 'invented' the black dog, Carlo, who sat on my shoulder when I was cross and difficult as a child. He was so real to me that I can remember screwing my head round in an effort to see him because I was utterly convinced my father could see him.

Perhaps we all have a 'black dog' of our own who is really representative of the dark side of human nature and seeing him in phantom form helps us to come to grips with this side of ourselves. Be that as it may, black dogs are very much part of the unseen animal world.

In East Anglia he is so common that he has been named 'Old Shuck' or just as The Shuck Monster.

J. Wentworth Day in his book "*Ghost Hunters Game Book*" published in London in 1958 lists several instances of his appearance in The Eastern Countries of England in fairly recent times. Lady Walsingham reported seeing him in the 1920s and in 1946 a gamekeeper called William Fell saw him in Essex.

Stories of a ghostly black dog are also prevalent in the West country of England. In 1932 there was a spate of near accidents on the Torrington Bideford road as a number of motorists braked furiously to avoid hitting a black dog which, on investigation, appeared to have no substance. A van driver who travelled regularly along the road said he had seen it on several occasions.

The theory was put forward that the dog was actually travelling along the route of a prehistoric track that coincided at that point with the present-day road. A similar idea is firmly held in East Anglia that Black Shuck never crosses Parish boundaries. These boundaries go back many hundreds of years, in some instances even to pre-Christian times and it has been discovered in recent years that they frequently follow the lines of the mysterious leys.

Black Shuck, although described by those who have seen him as a sinister- looking creature of massive size with burning, fiery eyes, would appear to be quite a benign ghost. His habit of padding along behind foot-travellers on lonely roads which sometimes earns him the name of 'Padfoot' is not done with malicious intent but to protect the travellers from would-be robbers.

In the north of England we find stories of the phantom black dog taking on a more sinister aspect as he is said to only appear as a portent of death, like the demon dog of Herefordshire who is said to appear to members of the Vaughan family as a warning of death.

Headless hounds appear to be a Cornish tradition. A midnight hunter accompanied by headless hounds apparently rides the Abbots Way on Dartmoor and Sir Francis Drake has been seen driving a hearse through Plymouth accompanied by headless - but still howling – hounds!

Stories of spirit dogs manifesting themselves to beloved owners after death are often a good deal more believable than ghost stories featuring dogs, and certainly a great deal more comforting.

One of the most extraordinary is the story of the dead dog who appeared in a photograph. William Hope of Crewe in England, was both a photographer and a medium. He combined his gifts by taking photographs of people and, quite frequently, a shadowy likeness of a dead relative would appear in the picture. He worked with another medium, Mrs Buxton, whose psychic power gave him added power in his work. One day she asked him to take a portrait of her family, in the hope that her recently dead father would appear. What was their amazement when the photo was developed to see, not Mrs Buxton's father as the extra sitter but a very clear likeness of "Floss" her little smooth-haired fox terrier, sitting on the lap of one of the sitters. The little dog has passed on some time before the picture was taken.

A delightful story of a Ghost, or spirit dog is told by the Australian psychic and clairvoyant, Maureen Dalziel in her booklet "*My Story*" (published by Broomtail Publications). She tells how unexpectedly having to walk home in the dark one night she was feeling really scared when she felt something against her legs, looking down she saw a beautiful Labrador dog. It stayed with her until she reached her destination. She bent down to pat her new friend in thanks and found there was no dog!

Whether we call them ghosts or spirits; whether we believe in them or not, the tales of ghostly dogs are legion, maybe our belief or otherwise does not affect their reality; so often people will wind up the telling of a good ghost story with the words, "I still don't believe in it - even though I saw it!" Easiest perhaps just to accept, like Milton, who wrote in 'Paradise Lost' -

"Millions of Spiritual Creatures walk the earth,
Unseen, both when we wake and when we sleep".

Legends, stories and superstitions about ghostly cats abound and there are few people who have known and loved cats for many years and do not have at least one good cat ghost story to relate. The cat has quite a unique relationship with man. She does not worship him, like the dog. On the contrary she herself has been the object of worship when as Bast she was most sacred of all the animal deities of Ancient Egypt. She has not been trained to be a useful slave nor does she provide us with food and clothing. She is, and always has been, the cat who walks by herself. Her own person, aloof, mysterious, and by choice nocturnal. All prime ingredients for the powerful hold she undoubtedly has on our awareness.

Few creatures can have had more strong words and less neutral ones spoken and written about them. Cats can, and do, inspire almost slavish devotion, respect bordering on awe or they can be feared and hated and seen as the embodiment of evil. We have only to glance at the legends and stories, even the proverbs that have been handed down from one generation to another to see that.

'Cats have nine lives, but if you take one, the cat will haunt you'.

'Never drown a cat - the devil will take revenge'.

'A cat sitting on a grave shows that the 'occupant' is with the devil'.

These are just a few of the proverbs in common use that show how the cat is linked with the occult. And cats of course, usually black, are as closely linked with witches in our minds as stove-pipe hats, black cloaks, potions and broomsticks!

No-one has probably ever appreciated the psychic qualities of the cat as much as the Egyptians. Not only was she worshipped as a deity and thus immortal but credited with having special powers to assist us mere mortals to reach paradise and thus attain immortality ourselves.

The cat, it was believed, with her special powers and her remarkable eyes which gave her not only remarkable natural sight but the gift of second sight, was the only creature that could lead the souls of the dead safely through the underworld to paradise. Hence the custom not only of embalming and preserving the bodies of dead cats but of burying cat charms and amulets with the human dead.

The idea behind embalming was that the body would still be available when the dead person (or cat) awoke from the long sleep of death. These re-awakening bodies could then live again. Not only was the cat believed to assist, but was also given every assistance on her way to heaven. Cat effigies were often buried with mummified cats so that should anything by way of accident happen to the mummy the soul of the cat would have another vehicle to enter and so would not lose its chance of eternal bliss.

A very similar belief to that of the Egyptians has survived for many years in the members of a Malayan tribe. They believe that a cat must lead the way when a soul makes the weary journey through Hell to Paradise, sprinkling water on them as they pass through. The same people believe that if anyone should kill a cat they will be punished in the next life. The punishment being quite specific, the stacking and carrying of a tree trunk the thickness of a coconut palm for every hair the cat possessed!

Whenever an Egyptian temple was dedicated to the sun an image, or symbol of a cat was placed within it. Legend has always given great power to these images, more often malevolent than otherwise. One such story was written by the Cairo correspondent of the London Daily Express in August 1919 and concerns an Australian soldier who was invalided to Egypt from The Dardaneles. In Alexandria he met briefly and fell in love with a beautiful Greek girl. Invalided out of the army and back in Australia he found he could not forget her and eventually he returned to Egypt to search for her. Sad and unsuccessful he was about to return to Australia but before he left he decided to visit Luxor where he duly visited to the Temple of Karnak. On the sarcophagus of a mummy was the image of a cat, he found himself staring at this with a curious intensity and then something touched his leg, looking down he was astounded to see what appeared to be the image of the cat at his feet. It moved slowly away, followed by the man, eventually it ran into a house where the Australian came face to face with his lost Greek girl.

Some ten years earlier Lord Carnarvon who was an archaeologist was excavating in Egypt when he came across the large hollow wooden figure of a black cat which he recognised as the outer case for a real embalmed cat. It was painted all over with a black pitch substance and had baleful yellow painted eyes. He sent it back to his house where a servant put it in his room.

Returning himself late at night, he walked into it in the darkness scraping his shin, unable to find the matches and getting no answer to his summons for a servant he went in search of a light to find all the house-hold servants gathered round the butler who had been stung by a scorpion and in the delirious state he had passed into was begging to be saved from the grey cat that was pursuing him.

Lord Carnarvon finally went back to his bed, his room was now in full moonlight which fell on the black figure of the cat. He found it hard to sleep. The shadow of a tree playing across the cat's face seemed to scowl angrily at him; he could still hear the poor butler imploring all and sundry to remove the grey cat. He wondered about the people who, some three thousand years ago had fashioned the cat in front of him to house the preserved remains of a creature that had been half pet and half God. He began to imagine that the painted eyes glittered.

At last he dropped to sleep, only to be woken by a report like a gunshot. He jumped up, and as he did so a large grey cat sprang across the bed, digging its claws into his hand in passing, and vanished through the window.

The bright moonlight shone on the mummy case which had split open revealing the mummified cat it held - its bandages torn open at the neck. Leaping out of bed and hurrying to the window he saw, not the grey cat that had leapt out the window but his own pet tabby standing in the moonlit garden, bottle brush tail erect, back arched, ears flattened and spitting as if she had seen a host of demons.

The records of psychic research societies in England and America bulge with stories of phantom cats; the interesting point about so many of these cat ghost stories is that at the time they were seen they were not suspected of being anything but real life flesh and blood cats. Typical of these stories is one told by Norah Chesson in The Occult Review. She was a young girl at the time and had been sick in bed and had not left her room for a week. She was a bit disappointed not to see her pet cat but thought she was pre-occupied with her six week old kitten. Then one morning when she was convalescent "Minnie", to her delight, trotted in through the door of her room. She rubbed her head against her young mistress purring loudly and generally showing great pleasure at seeing her again before leaving through the open door.

Shortly afterwards a maid brought in her lunch and the girl told her how much better she felt, especially after Minnie's visit. "Minnie's been dead and buried for two days" the maid told her, "Your mother didn't want you told while you were ill".

A case of a cat haunting a house was reported in the *Journal of Psychical Research* (England) in 1926. The house was a very old one, 15th Century, but had a reputation for being haunted.

Both the husband and wife saw the cat, a large black fluffy one, several times but did not mention it to each other until they had a visitor who remarked to them that she had seen a cat about the house several times, as it did not seem to be theirs, to whom did it belong? Many of my cat-loving friends have told me how they have felt, very strongly, the definite 'presence' of their loved pets for some time after their physical death; some have been convinced they have heard them and a few said that they have seen them.

Many years ago we had a pretty little blue and white cat called "Dinky" in our cat family. She was a gentle soul who did not make her presence greatly felt among more extrovert members of our animal family. Maybe that is why she felt the need to make herself known after her death. More than once I opened the door to admit a mewing cat to find nothing there. Was it just my imagination that I seemed to see a mist of soft grey fur slide past my legs? Perhaps all ghosts are nothing more than the product of our imagination - on the other hand perhaps not; and if any creature has the power to show itself to us in the astral body then surely it must be the strange, fascinating, mysterious, psychic cat?

In 1908 the British Society for Psychical Research enquired into the story of a phantom pig in the village of Hoe Benham near Newbury in Berkshire.

On November 2nd in 1907, two young men named Oswald Pitman and Reginald Waud were painting in the garden of their house, Laburnum Villa, around 10 a.m. Pitman got up to speak to the milkman and saw his girlfriend, Clarissa Miles coming up the lane to join them in a painting session. Trotting with her like a dog was a large white pig. When he told Waud this the latter told him to tell Miss Miles to keep it out of the garden and be sure to close the gate securely. He was a keen gardener. However, when she reached the gate there was no sign of the pig and she firmly denied all knowledge of the animal.

Pitman however was so convinced that he had seen it that she agreed to walk back up the lane with him and ask some children she had passed if they had seen it. None had.

The following morning the milkman, pressed by a puzzled Pitman, signed a statement to the effect that he had not seen the pig, pointing out as he did so that the whole area was under a swine fever curfew and any stray pigs found wandering would have to be destroyed.

Pitman and Waud then left the district to live in London for a few months and while there reported the incident to the Society for Psychical Research. When they returned to Hoe Bernham in February it was to find that the story had been widely circulated and they were inundated with stories of previous phantoms in the area.

An old man named John Barratt told the story of how when he was a young boy in 1850 he was returning home with seven other men in a hay cart along the same lane when a 'white thing' appeared in the air. All the men with him saw it and also the horses for they went wild with fright.

The same John Barrett claimed that in 1873 he saw a creature like a sheep pawing at the ground, he took a blow at it with his stick but it disappeared.

Another man, Albert Thorne, said that in the autumn of 1904 he saw 'summat like a calf - with glowing eyes'. Another witness, unnamed, said that in January 1905 he saw what he took to be the curate's dog in the lane, thinking it had strayed he went to catch it when it appeared to change into a donkey, rearing up threateningly on its hind legs before vanishing.

All these farmyard ghosts were believed by local people to stem from the suicide of a farmer called Tommy King whose farm, demolished in 1892 had bordered on the lane.

Pittman, Waud and Clarissa Miles had one more experience of the phantom. While walking down the lane together Miss Miles suddenly claimed to feel as if she were suffocating and to be in the grip of an irrational fear, she felt, she said, the presence of an evil being, charged with malice. About the spot where Pitman had first seen the pig they all three heard an un-earthly scream. This convinced Waud, who had been sceptical from the first, that the ghastly animal really did exist.

In more recent times the stories of the Surrey Puma may or may not be accounts of a ghost. Many theories abound about this large mysterious cat seen constantly in rural areas of Surrey throughout the 1960's.

The animal was described as about the size of a Labrador dog but definitely feline, at one time in the mid-sixties so many accounts of sightings were given that a mass break-out from a zoo seemed the most likely explanation!

In 1964 Billy Davidson, a Canadian Ranger with experience of Puma tracking joined the armed farmers patrolling the woods after a series of incidents in which cattle were mysteriously frightened and even mauled. He did not find the 'puma' though he did find evidence of a big cat including a lair.

The first account of a large feline in the area actually appeared in William Cobbett's 'Rural Rides' written in the late 18th Century. This could - however be a description of a wild cat as these were certainly known in England at that time.

So many 'sightings' were reported in the mid-sixties that a police file was kept and a special cage constructed at Godalming Police Station with zoo and R.S.P.C.A. officials on hand to help catch the animal. In 1968 all this suddenly stopped, the police file was closed, with no less than 362 entries, and word was generally circulated that it had been shot by a local farmer.

If this was true then the event received scant publicity, certainly nothing to compare with that received by the supposed sightings. And no concrete evidence in the form of photographs etc, remains to prove the existence of the puma. The legend still lives on - a mystery big cat was reported near Guildford in 1980 and another at Hastings in December of the same year.

One theory is that the appearance of the mystery puma that prowled the Surrey Hills is in some way tied up with leys. In 1973 a survey of mystery cats, or ghost cats appearing in the Bournemouth area showed them all to lie close to leys.

People usually say, quite dogmatically, that they believe in ghosts or they do not. They are so positive that even those who claim to have seen a ghost will finish their account with the words - 'But I still don't believe it!'

The fact, however, remains that people think they see ghosts. Tom Lethbridge, perhaps better known for his work on dowsing, also did a great deal of research on what ghosts really are. Do we see the ethereal or astral body of the person or creature and if that is so, how do we explain away such things as ghostly London buses? Do we receive a telepathic message or impression from someone else and thus 'see' the ghost? Or is it perhaps that particularly strong events, happenings or even emotions can leave behind a sort of psychic photograph which, given the right conditions, can be picked up and thus 'seen' by someone else at a later date?

Lethbridge suggested that nature generates fields of static electricity in certain places, particularly near running water. These 'fields' are capable of picking up and recording the thoughts and feelings of human beings and other living creatures.

A similar explanation for the appearance of ghosts is that strong emotions leave some sort of photographic impression in the area which can be picked up by sensitive people at a later point in time so that they 'see' a ghost. Such a theory could explain the story of "Duffy" the ghostly donkey.

In the early 1950's Leon Weeks, an American archaeologist was exploring the Turkish coast researching and photographing for a television series. While in the area he decided to take a closer look at the battlefields of the Gallipoli Peninsular. Hoping to turn up some relics of the 1915-16 campaign he set up camp.

For the first few nights, nothing untoward happened. Then one evening as he stood in front of his open tent smoking a last cigarette, he saw a man clambering down a nearby slope leading a donkey. Over the donkey's back was slung, what appeared to be, a human load.

Dr. Weeks, as well as being a distinguished archaeologist, was also a donkey enthusiast. He studded out his cigarette and scrambled over the rough terrain toward the man and the donkey. To his surprise he could not find them and his shouts went unanswered.

At about the same time the following evening the sound of falling stones attracted his attention. On the hillside above him he could clearly see the leather boots of the other man slung across the donkey's back. He again shouted - and again received no reply. Next morning there were no signs of either the man, or men, and the donkey.

Each evening at about the same time they appeared, and each morning Dr. Weeks searched without success for some sign of his nightly visitor. He shrugged off the whole thing as some sort of mirage, stuck camp and returned to Troy to continue his research.

He might have completely forgotten the whole incident if he hadn't had his memory jogged. Several years later, in 1968, Dr. Weeks visited London and while there was invited to dinner with an English friend and his family. After dinner the conversation turned to stamp collecting and his host got up to show him his extensive collection of Australian commemorative stamps. One of these had been issued to celebrate the 50th Anniversary of the Gallipoli campaign in 1915. It immediately caught Dr. Weeks' eye for the design on the stamp depicted 'Simpson and his donkey' forever remembered for their heroic part in rescuing wounded soldiers at Gallipoli. 'Simpson' was in actual fact John Kirkpatrick, born at South

Shields in County Durham, England in 1892. He emigrated to Australia and served during World War 1 in the 3rd Australian Field Ambulance.

In 1915 while serving at Gallipoli he acquired a donkey which he called 'Duffy'; together they saved the lives of many wounded soldiers before Kirkpatrick (or Simpson - the name he chose to enlist under) was himself fatally wounded while going down Monash Valley on May 19th, 1915.

Dr. Weeks had never heard the story of Simpson and his donkey and would not have noticed anything remarkable about the stamp, had he not been struck by the similarity between the figures depicted on it and his nightly visitors when he himself was at Gallipoli.

Philadelphia Robertson wrote the following beautiful verse about Simpson. But this is about animals in the Spirit World - which is not quite the same thing as Animal Ghosts in this world and is another chapter.

> 'Would it seem strange to you
> If somewhere in Elysian Fields
> Dropping the herbage by a crystal stream
> Wandered the little ass, tall Simpson's friend?
> Or strange at all,
> If, down the hill, beneath the flowing trees,
> Came Simpson, singing, his brown hands
> With celestial carrots filled
> For his old friend?
> To me, not strange at all.
> Amidst the beauty of some shining sphere
> They surely move -
> Those deathless hosts of Christ like chivalry'.

Chapter Seven

The Animal Soul

If we believe that the spirits of men live on after death, then we must also believe that the same thing happens to the spirits, or souls of animals, presuming of course that we accept that animals have souls.

If we define the soul as that divine spark within each person that makes he or she the individual, different from every other individual, then we must accept that animals too have a soul. Animals, like us, are individuals with as distinct personalities as people.

Many years ago I bred pedigree cats and I never ceased to be amazed at the strong individual personalities displayed by each kitten in a litter by the time they were a few weeks old. They may look as alike as the proverbial peas in a pod, externally, their characters were always enormously varied. It was these individual traits of personality in fact that enabled me to distinguish one from another rather than any physical peculiarities.

Who indeed who has ever experienced the love and selfless devotion of a dog can doubt that there is something more behind those wonderfully expressive eyes than 'blood, bone and sinew'?

Many people whose lives have been enriched by their contacts with animals will agree with Axel Munthe when he wrote the following in the preface to his book "*The Story of San Michele*" in 1936 - "I have loved them (animals) and suffered with them my whole life. I have loved them far more than I have ever loved my fellow-men. All that is best in me I have given to them, and I mean to stand by them to the last and share their fate, whatever it may be. If it is true that there is to be no haven of rest for them when their sufferings here are at an end, I, for one, am not going to bargain for any haven for myself. I shall go without fear where they go, and by the side of my brothers and sisters from forest and fields, from skies and seas, lie down in merciful extinction in their mysterious underworld, safe from any further torments from god or Man, safe from any haunting dream of eternity".

If, as he says, his love for animals was greater than his love for his fellow men - sufficiently great in fact for him to be willing to give up eternity if they too could not share it with him, then it was indeed a very great love. For Dr. Munthe was renowned for the love and service he gave to his fellow-men in his life work as a doctor of medicine.

Once however we accept that animals as well as people have within them the divine spark of immortality when we have to also accept that this applies to all animals. We cannot say that dogs, cats and maybe horses have souls while those we like to eat, such as sheep and cattle, do not. And what of the wild creatures we like to use for sport - what of the so-called vermin?

Carrying our thought processes a logical step further we come to the myriads of flying insects and creepy-crawlies - in fact everything that has life. We can, in fact, go even further and begin to wonder about plants - they too have life.

Most people who wonder this far probably lean to the idea of a spiritual evolutionary progress. Each creature has its own group soul which in turn is part of the whole creative force whether you choose to call this The Creative Force, God or just Nature is up to you.

When any living thing dies it rejoins its group soul, but it always has the chance to evolve - to develop into an individual soul. By it's own individual act of heroism or unselfishness, through altruistic love, or even by being the best of its kind - whatever that may be - it can raise itself up from the group soul to individual status.

When we get to the so-called 'higher' animals with their close association with Man we can see how a strong bond of mutual love forged between two souls, one human and one animal, can help the animal soul to evolve. Love is the strongest force in the world so when such a bond is formed it is only reasonable to assume that it will not be severed by death and that animals we have loved in this life will be with us in the next.

A very simplistic, if rather selfish, argument for the survival after death of our animal friends is the one that for so many people Heaven would simply not be - Heaven without them!

We live today in a world where knowledge is king. It is not enough to believe, we need to know - to have proof. We are all of us 'doubting Thomas'. It is not enough to see the risen Christ we need to feel the wounds for ourselves.

It is this attitude which, I think, explains in part the move away from orthodox religions and towards more unorthodox or 'way out' philosophies. Many of these place less emphasis on dogma and blind belief and more on individual spiritual exploration, we must find things out for ourselves.

One of the religions that is comparatively new is of course Spiritualism with its pre-occupation with life after death or survival of the individual soul. Harold Sharp, a spiritualist, wrote in his book 'Animals In The Spirit World', - "Since there is no death in any form of Life your animal friends live on as surely as do your human friends. It is only the physical sheaf which has been discarded and buried". Comforting words for the countless people who have ever loved and lost a pet.

The fact that animal ghosts can be seen by people would seem to be proof of the survival after bodily death of our animal friends. Animals too have frequently made their presence felt at Seances and many mediums often like to have their animals with them when they hold seances as they say that the presence of the animal 'gives power'.

In her book *"When Your Animal Dies"* published by the Spiritualist Press, Sylvia Barbanell gives countless instances of animals appearing at seances, often quite unexpectedly, and making their presence known by some peculiar quirk of character to their erstwhile owner. She records one particularly convincing incident at a sitting being held by the well-known medium Charles Glover Botham. The materialised form of a large dog suddenly appeared, he bounded at the circle happily and with excitement then lapped up a bowl of water. Afterwards it was seen to be completely empty and not a drop spilt.

Many returning spirits speaking through mediums at seances have mentioned the animals in the Spirit World. As one, Andrew Wallace, speaking though a medium put it, "They live as long as your love lasts for them - after that they go to their own place". The English psychic and hypnotist Vic Stewart has recorded on tape an 'interview' with a woman regressed into a past life under hypnosis. This regression takes her right up to and through her death in a former life. On arrival in the next world she is met by her 'dead' mother who tells her that she will continue to work and outlines the choices, one of these is caring for the souls of animals who die.

This ties in with those who claim to have had out of body experiences in which they have travelled the Astral plane and have seen many animals as well as people there. Those, these people say, who have loved humans already there will live with them - others will wait for them to arrive, and need caring for in the waiting time. For yet others, the 'wild' animals there are special places.

The only 'proof', if you can call it that, of the survival of animal spirits is the testimony of those rare mystics who claim to experience out of the body spiritual journeys in the Astral plane and those who have seen the spirit forms of animals who have died.

There is a distinction between these and ghosts. Ghosts are usually spirits which, for some reason or other, are earth-bound. They are usually unhappy and the experience of seeing them is a frightening one.

Returning spirits which show themselves to someone (usually a loved one or someone close to a loved one) are not frightening, on the contrary they either give great comfort or are accepted quite naturally because it is not always realised that they are not actual flesh and blood at the time of their appearance.

In her book "when your animal dies', Sylvia Barbanell tells many remarkable stories of animal survival. One I think is of special interest because the participants did not claim any psychic powers, had no knowledge of Spiritualism and had never studied the subject.

A London solicitor had to visit a client in the country. She was a new client at the time and he had never visited her house before. On his return he told his wife about the beautiful dog the woman had. How it kept running in front of his client and stopping to look up into her face. "I don't know when I have seen a dog with such a beautiful head, or one that looked so devoted" he told her. Some time later the woman took a flat in London and both the solicitor and his wife had occasion to visit her there.

"What have you done with your dog" the solicitor asked. There was an uncomfortable silence before the woman answered, very abruptly "I have no dog".

Later when the solicitor's wife and the woman were alone together she apologised for her curtness, explaining that since the loss of a dearly loved dog some years ago in tragic circumstances she had never been able to bring herself to have another.

"What sort of dog was it" the solicitor's wife asked her. "A White Highland Terrier" was the reply. The solicitor and his wife left the flat to go home. They were barely out when he exclaimed to his wife "It's an odd thing about that dog, I'll swear I saw one when I visited her in the country".

"What sort of dog was it?" his wife asked for the second time that afternoon. And for the second time came the reply "A White Highland Terrier".

More concrete evidence of survival after death is in the extraordinary appearance of a dead dog in a photograph.

William Hope of Crewe was a noted psychic photographer. He himself had great gifts as a medium and he worked in collaboration with another medium, a Mrs. Buxton. Several members of Mrs. Buxton's family met together on one occasion to be photographed by William Crewe, it was hoped that when the photo was developed Mrs. Buxton's father, who had recently died, would appear in the picture.

However, when the plate was developed Mrs. Buxton was amazed to find that the 'extra' in the family photo was not her father, but her dead terrier, Floss!

It is not only dogs or even dogs and cats that manifest themselves after death. There are records of horses, monkeys, cows, pigs, budgies etc, making themselves known whether to their erstwhile owners or to mediums at public seances. In fact Harold Sharp, who himself was very well known as a medium, said:

"In my own mediumship I have seen quite as many animals manifest as human beings".

I can remember, many years ago when I was living in Oxford and was a member of a small writer's group. One evening a member brought along a friend who was a medium. This particular person knew no-one at the meeting other then the person who brought her but in the process of giving the most uncanny readings for several members she gave one young woman a message from her 'dead' father, adding that his beloved dog was with him. She then proceeded to describe the dog (which was a mongrel and therefore quite individual in appearance) in almost photographic detail, and with her hearer said, absolute accuracy.

Dawn Hill, author of the book "*Reaching For The Other Side*" expressed her belief to me that animals can stay with a beloved human for some time after death. "I had" she told me, "a beautiful cream Persian cat who was torn to pieces by a marauding dog and who still snuggles down in a cloud of white mist in my son's bedroom wardrobe at night. Daryl has also felt (and seen) her on his bed at night and has heard a sociable miaow or two, as have other visitors to our home, some of whom knew nothing about her".

In every case we see that in life there has been a strong bond of love between the human and animal soul, Sir Oliver Lodge who spent nearly sixty years of his life in psychic investigation wrote - "I have often been asked about the survival of animals. Well, affection is the most vital thing in life, and, like other vital realities, it continues, the universe is governed by love more than anything else, and no reality of that kind fades out of existence".

So much for the animals who, in this life, have been dearly loved 'pets'. It is not hard to believe that our love for them will enable them to survive. But what of the many hundreds and thousands of animals who never find human love and companionship in this life - what of them?

These animals can be roughly sub-divided into two classes, the domestic 'wild animals' - that is cattle and sheep who live out their lives in flocks or herds - and the true wild animals.

It is relatively easy, on the supposition that we also accept the immortality of the human soul, to believe that our beloved pets' unique personalities will not just be snuffed out when their physical bodies leave this earth. We believe this because we want to. It is totally illogical to believe in an afterlife for our dog, which we love, and deny the same possibility for the kangaroo in the bush or the steer in the paddock.

It is worse then illogical, it is rank selfishness. We want to believe our dog lives on because his affection and companionship has contributed to the happiness of our earthly life and we feel that his continued affection and companionship may be necessary to the complete happiness of our life on the next plane.

Cicely Hamilton in a delightful short story, 'A Kitten In Paradise' written many years ago tells of the drunken thief who one night picked up a starving kitten from the gutter and stole a can of milk from a neighbour's doorstep for it. Unhappily for him he was seen, reported to the police and ended up once more in prison. While he was there he vowed to kill the kitten if he ever saw it again; however by the time he came out the kitten had already been killed in a street accident and the drunken thief himself died shortly afterwards in a brawl.

On arrival at the Gates of Heaven where he found himself, the blackest of souls, kneeling before St Peter with the Holiest of all the Holy Angels standing at his right hand, he was turned away because no-one in Heaven had need of him. But even as Peter was saying "You cannot enter - because no-one in Heaven has need of you". The Holiest of all the Angels called - "Listen!" and when Peter listened he heard a very tiny little cry!

Then, as The Black Soul looked up from it's uttermost despair, the key was turned and the gate opened - and there stood on the threshold a kitten. To the kitten, the Black Soul, befouled with many sins, was more glorious than the Shining Ones who looked on the Face of the Father for it had saved it in the night of it's hunger and despair.

Then Peter said, "You may enter, since one of the blessed has need for you".

But the Black Soul shrank away from the open gateway and covered his face with shame for he remembered how he had planned to destroy the kitten.

But as he turned away muttering that he was not worthy, The Holiest of All The Angels said : "Until you came, Heaven was not Heaven to a child of God, without you it cannot know the fullness of joy; the Lord has need of you, to make glad the heart of his kitten".

This beautiful little story throws another light on animals in the hereafter. In fact it reverses the argument so often put forward by animal-lovers for the continuous survival of the souls of their animal friends, that Heaven would not be Heaven for them without their pets.

In this story it is taken for granted that the kitten enters Heaven and the man only gets there because his presence was necessary to make it Heaven for the kitten.

We can look forward to a reunion with our beloved dog; could we feel the same about an astral meeting with the souls of the myriads of animals that mankind has slaughtered to eat? Killed because their habitat was needed for houses or mining or - and this is probably the worst of all - he has hunted and killed for an hour or so of selfish entertainment.

It is quite a dilemma, but one we have to face. Either we accept the possibility of a heaven for all creatures or we decide quite categorically that our animal friends have no soul - as we understand it - that all they have is this one short existence.

If we accept the latter view then I would suggest that it behoves us even more to endeavour to see that this one precious life at least is worth living - not the hell on earth that is the lot of so many unfortunate creatures.

Mrs Gladys Osborne Leonard who was a very sensitive and gifted medium, tells the story in her book, "*My Life In Two Worlds*" of a mystical experience she had which made such an impression on her that she never ate meat again for the remainder of her life.

One night, she tells us in her book, she had the experience of leaving her body, not with the usual soaring motion but with a heavy weighted feeling, she found herself in a narrow dark street, and though she could now stand upright she did not wish to put her feet on the ground because of the mud and slime underfoot. She was crowded into this 'street' by dark gloomy buildings like stables, the doors of these opened into what appeared to be a big yard. Peering through one of these openings she saw that the yard was crowded with animals, cattle, pigs and sheep. They appeared to be dead yet somehow she knew they were alive.

As she looked on this scene, which she says was more horrible than anything she could imagine she heard a voice explaining to her that this place lay between earth and the astral planes and that the 'bodies' she could see were those of slaughtered animals recovering from the shock of sudden death.

She goes on to say - "In the very air round me was a most definite feeling of terrible fear, suffering, and blind resentment that was even more tangible than the building and walls". The voice went on to explain to her that as this terrible feeling of suffering and resentment lay so close to the earth it had a bad effect on the spiritual and mental atmosphere of the earth, affecting human life.

The whole subject of animals and the afterlife seems to be one that dredges up a good deal of illogical and weird thinking to say the least of it. Some theologians would have us believe that animals can have no soul - and therefore no hope of a future existence after this earthly life - because they are merely sentient creatures without any sense of self-hood. This is a statement I feel has to be challenged. Who is qualified to state, quite categorically, that an animal does not have a sense of self. Only those who are capable of remembering what it is like to be an animal. To do this one must have been one in a previous incarnation which fact in itself would be proof of the immortality of the animal soul - not it's non-existence!

I would also challenge the statement that animals do not have a sense of self. In fact I would say that in the higher mammals this sense is every bit as strong as in Man. Without such a sense it would be impossible for a dog to learn it's own name for instance.

Belief in the immortality of animals is neither new nor confined to sentimental old maids. The ancient Egyptians had cemeteries for their dead cats which were mummified in the same way as people. Reisner, the archaeologist describes a stone inscription above the grave of a dog dating from about 2,600 B.C. which states that it was buried with much pomp and ceremony, 'in order that it might continue after life the role it had performed so well for it's master in this'. It's role in this life being body-guard to a king.

Similar beliefs in the after life of animals are found in the cultures of many different peoples living in many different lands and times. Greek, Roman, Phoenician, Babylonian etc.

Moslems are told in the Koran that - 'No beast is there on earth, or fowl that flies - that shall not be gathered unto the Lord'. In modern English Literature too we have countless references to this belief. A good example is Robert Southey's well-known poem - "*On The Death of a Favourite Old Spaniel*"

> ...There is another world
> For all that live and move. A better one!

Arther Findlay in his book "*On The Edge of The Etheric*" says: Animals as well as human beings survive death". Perhaps the last word on this subject should be given to Axel Munthe who ends his classic autobiography 'The Story of San Michele' with an imaginary confrontation between his own spirit after death and a heavenly tribunal, composed mostly of learned doctors of the Church. He writes - "I wish St Francis were among my judges. I have loved him my whole life - I wish I could see him to ask him a question I have asked myself my whole life. Where do the souls of friendly animals go? Where is their Heaven?" He was assured by the Lord that — "In my Father's House there are many mansions. God, who has created the animals, will see to that. Heaven is vast enough to shelter them also".

Chapter Eight

Many Happy Returns

I find it very surprising how few people consider their pets (or animal friends as I prefer to think of them) in terms of 'coming back' or reincarnation. But surely if the soul essence which we feel is particularly our own self can return many times to inhabit different bodies and take on different personalities on the Earth plane then so can those other special soul essences which inhabit the rather different bodies of our animal friends?

If we ever think of ourselves as part of the animal world then it is certainly as the very top. We might be right, intellectually, but intellect has nothing to do with spirit; and what persists after death and returns to use another body for another lifespan is not intellect but soul, spirit, or just if we like 'essence'; the very special spark that makes you, you, and me, me. Everyone who has ever loved a dog knows that this unique something is every bit as much part of its being as any other quality it has.

Many people accept that animals can reincarnate but they do not accept transmigration; that is the movement of the soul from species to species or human to animal. This I think is largely due to the Superiority Complex from which we, as human beings, suffer so badly! We can accept that animals can go 'up' and become human but not that humans can go 'down' and become animals! There have been some notable exceptions however, Pythagoras for example frequently enjoined his followers to treat animals well for housed in the body might be the soul of one of their own deceased relatives!

Seth, the renowned spiritual entity channelled for many years by Jane Roberts had some interesting lights to throw on the whole subject of reincarnation and transmigration. He suggested that the soul was not a neat single package as we are inclined to believe but that it can be split up and portions added to other entities so that we may understand better what it is to be a dog, or even a tree. He discusses at length the possibility of existing in different realities at the same time. He has this to say about animal spirituality: "The consciousness that is within them is as valid and eternal as your own. The mechanics of consciousness are the same. They do not change for animals or men. A dog is not limited to being a dog in other existences." Food for thought.

Maggie (short for Magpie) was a little piebald mare I bought with a filly foal at foot. The foal, Feather was a most unusual colour, mostly white with buckskin markings on her face and a black tail. A tail which I joked looked as if it had been given to her by mistake.

She was a beautiful little creature, with a delightful nature. We all loved her. In due course she was broken in and ridden by my children, mostly by Max, my younger son. Ruth his twin sister had her own pony, a young grey gelding called Crispin.

At the time we were breeding a few children's ponies and had a bay and white skewbald pony stallion. We decided to run Feather with him for a few weeks. A decision that was to break our hearts.

When we took her away from the stallion we returned her to her own paddock and normal companions, among them Crispin. Twenty four hours later we saw Fleur staggering about, blundering into things, like a zombie, pursued by Crispin.

Hastily we removed from the paddock and put her in the relative safety of a stable while I called the vet.

Though there were no signs externally of injury he was convinced that she had either been kicked in the head or driven into something and hit her head. Whatever it was it was some sort of serious head injury.

After another 24 tortuous hours in which we fought desperately for her life and tried to prevent her injuring herself further as she blundered and fell into walls, our beautiful and much loved pony lay dead.

A week or so after this tragedy we turned another of our pony mares out with the stallion. This mare, Fairy, was a dapple grey who had already had several foals, all grey. Fairy was 'pure for grey", that is being the progeny of two greys herself she would always produce grey foals, whatever the colour of the stallion. We had already bred a lovely dapply grey colt from her from a Palomino stallion.

Eleven months after Feather died Fairy's foal was born. My husband was the first to see her. He fetched me from the house, simply telling me that Fairy had foaled. He refused to tell me anything about the foal, just saying "Come and look at it!"

I followed him anxiously, by now convinced there must be something wrong, or at the very least, odd, about the new foal.

When I reached the foaling paddock I could only stare in amazement as the new foal, most uncharacteristically, left it's mother's side to trot over and greet me.

It was my prosaic and down to earth farmer husband who broke the silence. "It's Feather!" he said in a tone of awe.

I gazed at the foal, equally awe struck. Our grey mare had produced a most unusual foal, her body was white, her face had buckskin patches and she had a funny black tail that looked as if it had been given to her by mistake!

We called the new foal Fleur, and for the first couple of weeks of her life she caused her mother some concern by always wanting to socialise with us, almost as if she remembered us! When the vet who had attended Feather saw her first he, too, was amazed. "It's incredible" he said "I have never ever seen another horse before with Feather's unusual colouring, now here is another, and by all the laws of genetics it should be impossible!"

Fleur grew up to be as delightful a character as Feather and as dearly loved but alas also not destined to be long-lived. All her life was spent with us. When I look through the family snapshots I can only tell which is Feather and which is Fleur by the ages of my children in the photos with them.

In my memory they tend to blur into one pony and I am convinced in my heart that when Feather's life was so rudely cut short she returned to continue her relationship with us. In her second incarnation she became Ruth's pony for by the time she was ready to be ridden Max had grown too tall to ride a pony who only stood about 12.3 hands at maturity.

An interesting sidelight to this story is that during Feather's life her greatest friend was Pepita, my 12 hand mule, herself a remarkable character who, when Feather lay dying in the stable crawled through the paddock fence to take up her vigil outside the stable door. When Fleur was born the friendship seemed also to be reborn for throughout Fleur's life her greatest friend was Pepita.

I sometimes think that if we had any doubts about whether or not Fleur was also Feather, Pepita did not.

If animals can sometimes be more knowledgeable about these things than we are then so can young children.

I have heard it said by people from India, a country where reincarnation is more or less taken for granted, that we should pay attention to young children between the ages of 2 and 4 years when they speak of such things for at this age they are still young enough to remember previous lives and old enough to put their memories into words.

My grandson was three years old when he took a copy of my book *Cats' Company* off the shelf and stood for a long time staring at the picture on the cover. A fairly small picture showing me with one of my best beloved cats, Sheba, in my arms. Finally he came to me and asked me what was the cat's name. I told him; once more he stood for a long time looking at the picture then looking into my face asked me slowly, carefully, and very seriously: "Did she have hands BEFORE she was a cat?"

I was somewhat floored by this extraordinary question but as it was obviously so serious and important to him I tried to answer in the same vein. "I'm not sure" I told him with absolute truth. "What do you think"?

Once more he subjected the photo to an intense scrutiny. Then once more looking into my face in the same intense way he said: "I think she did. I think she did". With a little sigh he took the book back and replaced it on the shelf before resuming the normal childish game that he had interrupted for this conversation.

As for me, I was one shaken Granny because what he had said tied in so strangely with a VERY clear and (I thought at the time) quite bizarre, dream I had a few nights after Sheba died.

In this dream, which was the sort of dream that remains quite clear in the mind ever after, Sheba had appeared looking her normal and beautiful self, she was a long-haired white cat. But as I looked at her she began to speak and to change before my eyes into a little girl of about 7 years old. She was wearing a white dress and her shoulder-length red-gold hair was drawn back from her face in an Alice band. It was her words that were so bizarre.

"I have had my last incarnation as a cat" she told me. "Next time you meet me I shall be your grand-daughter".

Crazy as the dream seemed, and convinced as I was that, should I mention it, I might find myself committed, I did tell my daughter, who has odd dreams herself and anyway knows I'm crazy! I was quite unprepared for the look on her face or for her to interrupt my description of the little girl to finish it herself.

"I've dreamt of that little girl too!" She told me.

I can only guess at the truth behind this; all of which as you can imagine provided me with a great deal of food for thought. What I believe is that our understanding of time and the various dimensions of this world and the next is very limited. Time, as a linear concept, probably does not exist at all so that the idea of many lives, one after the other, is wrong. In fact the many lives may all be happening at the same time but in different dimensions or on different vibrations and my small grandson had met, or knew, Sheba in a different dimension, one which she not only had hands but a human form.

I might add that I have not, to date, got a grand-daughter and maybe I am not even destined to meet Sheba in this form on Earth.

When we begin to think about Reincarnation there is always the very real danger that we may get so 'hooked up' on other lives that we will almost forget to live in THIS life! Similarly there is the danger that when we think too much about reincarnation and our animal friends we will fail to see the little person who is sharing our life today and only see the personality that was there before. So if we really think we are living with a 'born again' it is important to keep this belief in perspective or we may find that we are losing something very precious in our relationship with the present day manifestation of a much loved spirit.

I have mentioned love because this I am sure is the key factor influencing the return of a spirit; every soul has the choice to return and a strong bond of love is the biggest incentive of all.

Most animals who return make the fact known on two counts, a strong physical likeness, or perhaps just one outstanding and unusual physical trait, and something in their behaviour pattern that suggests memory rather than learning. I share my life now with a delightful feline purrson who I am convinced has shared at least one other life with me. Her story begins with her predecessor. Tabitha looked like a striped Blue Burmese; her coat was a soft grey/blue with tabby markings in a darker shade of the same colour. She had large ears, a longish tail, a head reminiscent of Pasht, the sacred cat of Egypt, a deep full throated Siamese voice, a keen intelligence, a loving heart and a deeply rooted conviction that she was not as other cats! Her mother was a Tonkinese (a cross between a Siamese and a Burmese) her father a 'travelling man'.

She was very special, but no saint! During her life she caught, killed and ate my beloved budgie friend and terrorised and unmercifully bullied one of our other cats, Lucy. Ironically I only had Tabitha as a kitten to be a companion to Lucy! She was an inveterate rabbiter (we then lived out in the bush) and used to take herself off on hunting expeditions that sometimes lasted for days. Often she returned in the wee small hours, yelled at my bedroom window and snuggled down in bed with me, wriggling round so that her head was the same way up as mine and I would drop back to sleep with her happy purr thrumming through my consciousness. She taught herself to open the pantry door, the only cat among a great many who did, and also to remove the lid of the dog-meat saucepan and help herself – again the only cat who did. She never ate raw meat (other than the rabbits she caught) but loved the same meat cooked. I had an ongoing joke with her, "when you come back next time - "I would say, "Just be sure you LOOK like a Siamese so that everyone can see at a glance you are special!"

Then I dreamed a dream; Tabitha was away on one of her expeditions, she had been gone 3 days but I was not seriously worried as she had been known to stay away for as long as 10 days and come home safely. But in my dream Tabitha, moving in a sort of golden aura, was walking towards me and saying "Don't worry about me; I'm all right!" Just that, nothing more.

I woke and told my husband; "Tabitha is dead, we shall never see her again!": The dream had been so clear I knew that her spirit had spoken directly to mine. I was right, I neither saw nor heard anything of her again.

It was about six months later when I first heard about the beginnings of Tara. A friends was regaling me over coffee with the rather long-winded story of a young friend of hers who had lost her lovely Siamese cat. An advertisement in the paper did not result in her finding her own cat but another lost Siamese female.

Alas this second cat had proved to be in kitten and her new owner lived with a stepfather who only allowed her one (well-behaved) cat. Her lost cat had been spayed. The kittens duly arrived; six of them, five were black and white and the sixth pure white. Some weeks later when I met my friend again I got an up-date. The pure white kitten had developed Siamese colouring; all the Black and White ones had found homes but no-one wanted the Siamese! She had advertised in the paper, asked all the Pet Shops, all to no avail. I listened sympathetically, but I had a full house of cats, all of whom had come to me in need at some time in their lives. I didn't need another cat. Then my friend phoned; her young friend was desperate, the Siamese kitten was now four months old and step-father had decreed that one cat had to go. I agreed to go and look at her! The upshot of course was that Tara came home with me in exchange for a copy of my book *Cats' Company*.

It was just before lunch on Sunday, Mother's day, that Tara and I met. By afternoon tea time of the same day she had opened the pantry door and helped herself to cat biscuits, just as Tabitha always did, and had climbed up onto the electric stove by exactly the same rather circuitous route that Tabitha always took, lifted the lid off the dog meat saucepan and sampled the contents. Two things which no other cat had learned to do. This was so surprising that my somewhat sceptical husband made the comment; "That cat seems to have been born knowing what it took Tabitha two years to learn".

As time went on and she settled into the household other typical Tabitha traits emerged. She would never touch raw meat, and nine years down the track still won't, but loves the cooked dog meat. She wriggles down the bed and turns round so that her head is the same way up as mine, just as Tabitha did, and she continued Tabitha's vendetta against poor Lucy; so much so that in the end my daughter took Lucy to live with her. There is one notable exception; she has never shown any desire to hunt rabbits. I feel that as Tabitha met her end on a rabbiting expedition some important lesson may well have been learned!

Another interesting point is that when Tabitha first came to live with me she was shocked to learn that she was expected to share the house with dogs. Where she came from dogs were kept securely chained! During her lifetime she quite got over her dislike of dogs. Tara, who had lived with only humans and her mother, accepted the dogs with no trouble and in fact is now so attached to one of them that she goes out of her way to rub round her, purring to show her affection.

Another odd point is that over the years Tara's Siamese appearance has changed to the subtly muted Siamese 'look' of a Tonkinese, and in fact people who have these lovely cats have assured me that is what she is. But certainly everyone can see by her appearance that she is 'special' for, like Tabitha, she is convinced that she is something quite apart from other cats!

I have no doubts that Tabitha has returned to me, this time looking as I so often said she must, like a Siamese. I often think of the extraordinary chain of events that brought her to me; how she could look, as I suggested, like a Siamese but have no papers and be of no real monetary value; for with a house already full of cats I was unlikely to go out, cheque book in hand, and buy a Siamese kitten. Not the least I ponder the oddity that while her black & white siblings found homes so easily no-one would have her.

We often bewail the short physical lives of our animal friends, but there is one advantage, during our longer life they can come back to us again, and may-be even again, giving us a wonderful opportunity to enjoy their Many Happy Returns!

Chapter Nine

And What Now?

When you kill a beast say to him in your heart,
"By the same power that slays you, I too am slain;
and I too shall be consumed.
For the law that delivered you into my hand shall
deliver me into a mightier hand.
Your blood and my blood is naught but the sap
that feeds the tree of heaven".

Kahlil Gibran.

As our world moves forward into a New Age it seems to me, in spite of the prophesies of doom and gloom, even in spite of the dark shadow of nuclear war, we are slowly gaining wisdom.

Wisdom and knowledge are not always the same thing, alas. Knowledge mankind has a-plenty, the wisdom to use it often seems terribly lacking. It is our knowledge that threatens to destroy us and our world, unless we can find the wisdom to use it correctly.

Many so-called primitive peoples of the world, not least the Aborigines of Australia, have deep wells of this wisdom which, instead of tapping, the 'advanced' races, have systematically ignored and suppressed. As a result the more our technology advances, the more perilously near we bring ourselves and our whole planet to the brink of destruction.

A very simple example of this can be seen in Australia. For 30,000 years the Aborigines lived here, in harmony with their environment, able to live in and off the land as it was. They did not destroy their environment but lived with it. A mere 200 years of white settlement has changed the face of the country and brought about serious ecological problems.

However, the fact that we recognise these problems is surely hopeful? Not only do we recognise them but we have people trying to do something about it.

In spite of the destruction, the wars and the senseless cruelty in the world, I look to the future with hope for it seems as if, eight hundred years after his death, the spirit of St Francis is once more abroad.

If not the saint himself, then surely some great cosmic mind force is infiltrating the consciousness of thinking and caring people everywhere. People are realising that planet Earth is not the exclusive property of Man to despoil and destroy as he sees fit.

It cannot be mere chance that the same ideas and ideals spark off so many minds at once.

Our burgeoning 'whale consciousness' is one example. Quite suddenly, or so it seems, people all over the world have become aware of whales and dolphins. Aware of them not, as hitherto, as a 'resource' to be exploited to the full, but as co-inhabitants of this world of ours.

As a result of the extensive studies made of dolphins we are not only aware of their remarkable intelligence and brain power and complicated social structure but are beginning to realise that they just may have something to teach us about living together in peace and harmony without destroying our own environment.

The Green Peace Movement and the Down to Earth Movement also show a large scale turning back to and caring for our environment.

The fact that the great move back to a more simplistic lifestyle closer to Nature involves so many young people is surely heart-warming.

These people have not only become sickened by the artificiality of modern life in the urban 'concrete jungle' but are aware that the devastation and wastage of our vital natural resources that such a way of life entails, can bring in the end nothing but disaster and destruction, both on an individual and global scale.

For many of them a return to a more simple way of life also means that they gain a much greater knowledge and understanding of the animal world. This, surely, must ultimately be to the benefit of both.

As we move forward into the New Age, searching for our Spiritual identity in a way that it seems mankind has seldom done before in our study of old and new religions in and from East and West, perhaps we will also become increasingly aware of the animals as spiritual creatures?

For all too long Man has been dependant on the animals not only as co-workers and a source of power and energy but for clothing and food.

With advancing technology it is possible that the day could be in sight when all this could change. With the great strides that have been made in the last half-century or so in the manufacture of man-made fabrics we no longer need to exploit them for clothing. The day may not be too far away when we no longer eat them.

Vegetarianism in the Western world is on the increase. Although alas, it must also be conceded that we in the West have 'sold' the idea of eating meat to many of our Eastern friends.

The spread of vegetarianism in the West is due to a number of factors. Not the least is the high cost of meat allied to rising living costs outstripping wage rises, and increasing unemployment.

Of recent years many people have been taking a new look at our traditional ideas on health and nutrition and many have come to the conclusion that a diet that is predominantly a meat one is not in the best interests of sound health.

There are also a growing number of thoughtful, intelligent people who care about the world's starving millions and realise that it is simply bad economics to use so much of the precious land resources of the world to keep animals which are only kept for their carcass value.

Not only are these animals occupying valuable farming land themselves but vast tracts of cultivable land are used to grow crops to feed them. In terms of simple economics this is gross waste. If this land was used to grow food for human consumption far more protein could be produced than when this food is channelled through animal bodies to appear on the world market as meat for those who can afford it.

Lastly but by no means least there is a vast number of people, a growing number, who, in their search for spiritual enlightenment become convinced that the eating of the flesh of animals, our co-tenants of Earth is just 'not on' in an ethical sense. Many people as they evolve spiritually become sickened by the disgusting practices of modern factory farming before they finally reach this conclusion.

Hens for instance, de-beaked to prevent them devouring their neighbours in a kind of frenzy of boredom, doomed to spend their short lives in cages so cramped and small they can scarcely move, on wire floor which make the possibility of ever being able to scratch for food or enjoy a dust-bath a totally unattainable dream. Fed, by mechanical conveyor belt, a concentrated food in pellet form designed to produce optimum efficiency, and kept for lengthened days in artificial light for the same reason, they are reduced to mere egg-laying machines.

Anyone who has ever kept free-range hens will understand fully the reduced circumstances of these unfortunate creatures. The free-range hen living a natural life has a life-expectancy of 8-10 years instead of about 2 at the most for the battery hen.

She will be busy for most of her waking hours, scratching happily around for food, she will enjoy a social life with her fellows where such things as cannibalism are unknown and moreover she will lay during her life-time a good quota of eggs, which I am sure are far healthier and with better food value than those laid by her unfortunate sisters serving a life sentence of the battery system.

We have always kept sufficient free-range hens to keep the family in eggs, but once, when we were low on numbers we purchased six hens who were being sold off cheap for eating from a local poultry farm.

What a sorry sight they were, de-beaked and with colourless drooping combs and messy looking feathers. They looked like old hens yet by our standards they were little more than pullets. But even more pathetic than their appearance was their behaviour. Each morning when the chook house door was opened out ran our original hens, squawking with joy and scratching like mad. The behaviour of the battery hens was in marked contrast, they stood in the doorway of the hen house surveying this extraordinary world, and no doubt marvelling at the courage and temerity of the chooks who inhabited it, then retreated to the safety of the interior of their new home. No doubt even this seemed immensely spacious to them after their battery.

Gradually as the weeks went by, first one and then another timidly stepped over the threshold. It was six months before they all really enjoyed coming out and exploring their new world and about as long before they began to look like happy healthy chooks.

I have often thought that their experience could be likened to that of the soul who does not realise for some time yet it has, in fact, left its earthly body and is now in heaven!

The battery system of poultry farming has been outlawed in some enlightened countries. In Australia to our shame it is not. And yet, God knows, in this vast country we have land to spare surely for our chooks to have a little freedom and to gain at lest some pleasure from their brief lives?

So-called 'Progressive' methods of raising calves and pigs in intensive indoor units where they never see the light of day until they are taken out to be killed are even more repugnant to the thoughtful person. Even to the health fanatic, all too often these unfortunate animals are pumped full of serums and antibiotics to keep them 'healthy' and with hormones and special growth stimulants to reduce still more the time between their birth and their inevitable early death and increase still more the profit margin of those whose 'living' is the death of their fellow creatures.

Our exploitation of animals does not, of course begin and end with eating them.

Millions of animals are bred, reared and killed for their fur coats, millions more are trapped and die in excruciating agony for the same purpose. Before Man had developed the 'know how' to make synthetic furs there may have been some excuse for this in extremely cold regions. Now when simulated furs can be as warm and beautiful as the real thing and are, moreover, moth proof there can be no possible excuse for spoilt and selfish women to use the skins of other creatures to enhance their own beauty. Apropos of this - it has always seemed to me the ultimate in blasphemy when I have seen a woman wearing a fur coat in church, the more so if she truly believes she is there to pay homage to He who is Love incarnate.

The most obscene cruelty inflicted on the animal world by man is undoubtedly the practice of vivisection. The word vivisection means - just that. The cutting up of living creatures. The fact that it is done in the holy name of science - for the ultimate good of mankind can in no way justify such wholesale cruelty and callous misuse of God's creatures.

When, as Prof. H.F. Harlow wrote in the journal of comparative and physiological psychology, "Most experiments are not worth doing and the data obtained are not worth publishing" then one can only conclude that, at best, vivisection is a means of providing employment, at worst of satisfying the love of cruelty that, alas, is there in most of us.

A very typical example of a totally useless experiment for psychological research was done when rats were first blinded, then deafened and finally deprived of their sense of smell to see how they learned to negotiate a maze. Not surprisingly, it was found they had little ability to learn.

A totally pointless experiment in the physiological field was the use of pregnant baboons to see if the use of seatbelts could contribute to foetal deaths. This was done after it had been discovered that the wearing of seat-belts by pregnant women could have this effect.

As the general public is not kept informed of the money spent on experiments on animals and few countries publish statistics, it is difficult to gauge with any degree of accuracy just how many animal lives are sacrificed annually. A conservative estimate however for America alone is approximately eighty million a year of which about 250 thousand are monkeys, 250 thousand dogs, 100 thousand cats and the remainder small animals, guinea pigs, rats, mice etc.

The number of primates (monkeys) used annually in the vivisection laboratories of the world is increasing so rapidly that at least nine Asian and eight African species are in danger of extinction. Is this really the way God expects Man to exercise his dominion over the animal world? Apart from the appalling nature of the experiments themselves in many cases, often done without anaesthesia, the life of an animal imprisoned in a wire cage in a laboratory is scarcely what it was created for.

Those who value human life, and the prolonging of it, above all else may well argue the case that the practise of animal experimentation is permissible, even laudable, if it will help in attaining that end. But Christians also teach, and one presumes, believe, that this life is merely a prelude to a fuller and better life in another world. If that is so then why do we need to go to such extreme lengths to promote our life here on earth?

There can be no argument however in favour of cruel experiments done in the name of beauty. Many experiments are done in the field of manufacturing cosmetics such as putting shampoo in rabbit's eyes to see if it blinds them. The shampoo used was so strong that the eyes were dissolved and the experimenters had their answers.

Neither can there be any justification for tests to find out the effects of cigarette tar. It is already widely known that smoking is harmful and excessive cigarette smoking can cause cancer so why on earth should the lives of innocent animals, who anyway are not so foolish as to mal-treat their own bodies in this way, be sacrificed merely to prove that is already known.

Those who argue in favour of vivisection take the line that animals are sub-human, they cannot speak and defend themselves therefore they have no rights. I would suggest that it is only a small step before we use other 'sub-human-creatures, babies born hopelessly retarded who, like animals, cannot speak and defend themselves.

Many thinking people today hold the view that no real and lasting good can ever come through vivisection. In fact quite the reverse. By our callous infliction of suffering on other sentient creatures who share this planet with us we are merely adding to the dark pool of evil and misery and that we - as a species - cannot hope to gain light, or enlightenment, or even worthwhile knowledge, from such a source.

"The Kingdom of Heaven Is Within You" - famous words from the greatest teacher and healer of all time. Healing too comes from within; no amount of scientific experimentation on animals will heal the ills of mankind, we have to look within ourselves.

Appalling experiments have been going on throughout the world for many years on an ever-increasing scale to find a cure for and treatment of cancer, if such a cure were found, overnight it would probably cause as much havoc and ruin as the disease itself!

If we were to turn our energies towards ourselves, alter our whole way of life, our way of thinking, perhaps we could begin to see some light at the end of the tunnel.

As we approach the year 2,000 and the world enters a New Age, the Aquarian age, I think, in spite of the arms race, the quarrelling over ideologies between nations, the very real threat of nuclear war and total holocaust, in spite of all this there is cause for hope.

The New Age is believed to be bringing with it a new spiritual awareness. Religion will become less a thing of church building and dogmas and more what it was always meant to be, an inner knowing.

There are heart-warming signs that this is indeed so. Nowhere is this more clearly demonstrated than in our relationships with the other creatures who share the earth with us.

A growing number of people are becoming increasingly aware that animals - as well as people - have rights. Moreover they are prepared to stand up and be counted, to speak out and defend those rights.

The dilemma that faces mankind today is that his intellectual achievements have far outstripped his spiritual growth. A deeper understanding and caring for our animal friends may go a long way to redress the balance.

Man's intellect has taken him even beyond the bounds of his home planet. We dream of establishing contact and understanding with beings from other worlds then our own. Before we do that, perhaps we should establish real contact and true understanding of the other creatures who share our own earth. The rewards could be greater than we imagine.

Cats' Company - A book of cats & - history -- healing - communication - stories by

Ann Walker

Ann explores the role of the cat through history, from being worshipped in Ancient Egypt to being cruelly treated and hated in Medieval Europe. The book includes tales of cats who returned to their owners after death, both in spirit and reincarnated form. Stating that "The Ancient Celts believed that the eyes of a cat were windows through which humans could explore the inner world", we are given an extract from a grimoire giving guidance on how to attune yourself to your cat. Believing in the healing power of cats and our ability to think/talk with them, Ann shares many stories of the cats she has known and loved over the years. A fascinating and enthralling book for cat lovers everywhere.

ISBN 1898307 32 6   £10.95

Your Talking Pet by Ann Walker

Your Talking Pet is about 'companion animals', the cats and dogs who live in our houses and are called 'pets'. For various reasons, we selected these two species to share our homes and our lives and the result is a mutual dependency; they on us for their well-being, we on them for companionship, love and even to boost our self esteem. Sometimes there is a total misunderstanding between us, at others we share a bond that is as strong as any we have with our own kind. Packed with interesting facts and real-life stories, some funny and some sad, this book about people and pets will strike a chord in the heart of everyone who has ever lived with, and loved, a cat or a dog.

ISBN 1898307 873   £8.95

Sacred Celtic Animals by Marion Davies

Animals affected the everyday lives of the Celts. The Celts saw animals as representations, representatives and messengers of their deities. They took animal names for themselves and their tribes and saw portents and auguries in animals' movements and behaviour. Animals featured extensively in Celtic legends and decorated their weapons, houses and accoutrements. Celtic shamans linked with animals and their warriors and hunters invoked the power of totem animals to help in their endeavours. This book details the myths, legends and correspondences linking the Celts and the animal world. Brilliantly illustrated by Simon Rouse.

ISBN 1898307 75X   £11.95

Sacred Animals by Gordon Maclellan

This is a book about animals, animals to wonder over in the Otherworld and in this physical world. Communicating, organising a sacred space, using words and chants, finding totems, the use and making of masks and costumes, body paints, music and dance are all part of communicating with animal spirits. These are all described here together with practical issues such as conservation and the integration of magic, ritual and practical hands-on action. Gordon communicates his love and wonder of animals, and of life with the enthusiasm and vitality for which he is widely known - a brilliant book full of practicality and feeling.

ISBN 1 898307 69 5   £9.95

The Intuitive Journey by Ann Walker

The journey in this book is, of course, the one from birth to death. During the course of a lifetime we have many different bodies, differing in size and appearance, yet our inner view of ourselves may change little from childhood to old age. Much has been written about developing psychic powers. The author sets out to prove that it is not a question of a favoured few developing special qualities, but of removing the blocks to using the gifts each one of us has been given to help us on what should, indeed be an intuitive journey.

ISBN 1898307 865   £8.95

FREE DETAILED CATALOGUE

A detailed illustrated catalogue is available on request, SAE or IRC appreciated. **Titles can be ordered direct from Capall Bann, post free in the UK** or from good bookshops and specialist outlets. We have over 200 titles currently available including:

A Book of Beasts by Nigel Pennick
Arthur - The Legend Unveiled by C Johnson & E Lung
Auguries and Omens - The Magical Lore of Birds by Yvonne Aburrow
Book of the Veil The by Peter Paddon
Caer Sidhe - Celtic Astrology and Astronomy by Michael Bayley
Cats' Company by Ann Walker
Celtic Lore & Druidic Ritual by Rhiannon Ryall
Compleat Vampyre - The Vampyre Shaman: Werewolves & Witchery by Nigel Jackson
Crystal Clear - A Guide to Quartz Crystal by Jennifer Dent
Earth Harmony - Places of Power, Holiness and Healing by Nigel Pennick
Earth Magic by Margaret McArthur
Enchanted Forest - The Magical Lore of Trees by Yvonne Aburrow
Familiars - Animal Powers of Britain by Anna Franklin
Healing Homes by Jennifer Dent
Herbcraft - Shamanic & Ritual Use of Herbs by Susan Lavender & Anna Franklin
In Search of Herne the Hunter by Eric Fitch
Magical Incenses and Perfumes by Jan Brodie
Magical Lore of Cats by Marion Davies
Magical Lore of Herbs by Marion Davies
Mysteries of the Runes by Michael Howard
Patchwork of Magic by Julia Day
Psychic Self Defence - Real Solutions by Jan Brodie
Runic Astrology by Nigel Pennick
Sacred Animals by Gordon MacLellan
Sacred Grove - The Mysteries of the Forest by Yvonne Aburrow
Sacred Lore of Horses The by Marion Davies
Sacred Ring - Pagan Origins British Folk Festivals & Customs by Michael Howard
Seasonal Magic - Diary of a Village Witch by Paddy Slade
Secret Places of the Goddess by Philip Heselton
Talking to the Earth by Gordon Maclellan
Taming the Wolf - Full Moon Meditations by Steve Hounsome
The Goddess Year by Nigel Pennick & Helen Field

Capall Bann is owned and run by people actively involved in many of the areas in which we publish. Our list is expanding rapidly so do contact us for details on the latest releases.

Capall Bann Publishing, Auton Farm, Milverton, Somerset, TA4 1NE
Tel 01823 401528   Fax 01823 401529   Email: enquiries@capallbann.co.uk